"I have known and worked closely with Richard Woods for over 20 years. In my opinion, he is one of the top wildland fire investigators in the world. He has played an integral role in both the development and the international delivery of the National Wildfire Coordinating Group's wildfire investigation training and certification packages and accompanying guidebook. This book that Richard has authored, is an excellent introduction and overview of these advanced wildfire investigation practices and an important addition to the fire investigator's bookshelf".

— **Mr. Paul Steensland**, *United States Forest Service Law Enforcement and Investigations, Senior Special Agent, (ret.), Oregon, USA*

"As the global community grapples with the immense challenges brought about by a changing climate that continues to increase the intensities and frequencies of wildfires, not only in traditional fire prone areas across the world, but in new areas where fire has not previously been experienced, the authoring of this Wildfire Arson Prevention Guide is both timely and essential. This is the first time that such an array of knowledge, skills, and experience have been brought together under one cover to reveal how individuals, agencies, and governments who are responsible for the protection of citizens and communities from wildfire can improve their competency and confidence in understanding their causes. It is only by getting to the root cause of ignitions and putting in place strategies and programs to minimise their occurrence can we be confident that climate extremes conducive to catastrophic fire weather conditions do not result in catastrophic wildfires. I highly commend this Guidebook to anyone who has a professional or personal interest in building safer communities in the face of such an overwhelming force of nature. Richard's experience and wisdom gained over more than 40 years is infused throughout and his methodological approach greatly assists in making a complex science easy to understand and even easier to implement".

— **Dr. Mark Crosweller AFSM**, *Founder and Director Ethical Intelligence, N.S.W, Australia*

"Richard Woods has written an easily accessible book, designed to assist law enforcement and fire agency personnel responsible for addressing the cause of wildfires. This guide is about proven practice and practical approaches. It is designed specifically for wildfire investigators tackling the problem of serial wildfire ignitions. The tone is instructive and Richard certainly has the credibility in this specialist field. After many years of investigating wildfires and training officers, he is recognised as Australia's preeminent authority on wildfire investigation and thus represents Charles Sturt University as an adjunct lecturer, providing opinion on the cause of wildfires. You will find this guide a valuable tool and I highly recommend it to investigators in the field of wildfire investigation".

— **A/ Professor Valerie Ingham**, *Associate Professor of Emergency Management, Charles Sturt University, N.S.W, Australia*

Wildfire Arson Prevention Guide

Wildfire arson is often considered an impossible crime to solve. Likewise, offenders frequently consider themselves undetectable. Many agencies often do not have the specialist skills necessary to investigate those responsible for serial wildfire ignitions. As such, perpetrators continue to light fires with little to no likelihood of being caught. An ongoing series of deliberately lit wildfires can result in significant financial and environmental consequences and put life and property at risk.

This *Wildlife Arson Prevention Guide* provides law enforcement, land management and fire agency investigators with frameworks, strategies and tactics—that can be adopted to address deliberate wildfire ignitions in their jurisdiction. Often this crime is automatically given to law enforcement agencies to solve in isolation, whereas a collaborative approach across key agencies has proven essential in apprehending offenders.

This valuable guidebook fills a void in the literature, detailing a collaborative approach through the adoption of successful best practice investigation techniques. Many may be applicable to—and better serve—smaller rural communities, while others can be adopted in more populated wildfire-prone areas. This book recognises that some small rural agencies may have less capacity to address the issue and may need to modify the recommended methods; ideally, the text encourages the establishment of collaborative arrangements to work with larger or adjoining agencies, to help solve their serial wildfire arson cases. This book highlights successfully adopted measures that can be embraced by key agencies that have a responsibility for wildfire ignition prevention.

Currently, no similar all-encompassing handbook exists to guide agencies to address this growing worldwide problem. The strategies and tactics are presented in a format that can be easily aligned to jurisdictions within countries that are at risk of wildfire. The commonly recognised motives behind wildfire arson are detailed to provide agency investigators with a background to this often-misunderstood offence.

The *Wildlife Arson Prevention Guide* provides the tools that will help authorities to identify those responsible and result in stronger, safer communities.

Richard Woods AFSM has had 39-year career initially in law enforcement and later in rural fire management in Australia. He established the fire investigation capability for the NSW Rural Fire Service and as a long-term member of North American National Wildfire Co-ordinating Group Wildland Fire Investigation Sub Committee, introduced the Wildland Fire Investigation Case Development Course to Australia. In 2010, as Co-Chair of the National Bushfire Arson Prevention Working Group, he developed Australia's Bushfire Arson Prevention arrangements. He is an Adjunct Lecturer in Wildfire Investigation with Charles Sturt University and is the Director of an international consultancy, 'Wildfire Investigations and Analysis'. He is the current Chair of the International Association of Arson Investigators Wildland Fire Investigation Committee. In 2013, he was awarded the Australian Fire Service Medal for his commitment to wildfire investigation. He holds a Graduate Diploma in Fire Investigation and a Graduate Certificate in Applied Management.

Wildfire Arson Prevention Guide

Richard Woods AFSM

CRC Press
Taylor & Francis Group
Boca Raton London New York

CRC Press is an imprint of the
Taylor & Francis Group, an **informa** business

Designed cover image: Photograph by the author

First edition published 2023
by CRC Press
6000 Broken Sound Parkway NW, Suite 300, Boca Raton, FL 33487-2742

and by CRC Press
4 Park Square, Milton Park, Abingdon, Oxon, OX14 4RN

CRC Press is an imprint of Taylor & Francis Group, LLC

ISBN: 9781032405964 (hbk)
ISBN: 9781032405940 (pbk)
ISBN: 9781003353843 (ebk)

DOI: 10.4324/9781003353843

Typeset in Minion
by codeMantra

Contents

Foreword **ix**
Acknowledgements **xi**
About the author **xiii**

Introduction **1**

Why is wildfire arson assumed to be difficult to address? 2
How big is the issue of wildfire arson? 3
Intent of this guidebook 4

1 Recognised wildfire arson motives **7**

Commonalities of behavioural motive models 11
Conclusion 14

2 The wildfire arson investigation challenge **17**

The 'hidden problem' of the extent of wildfire arson 18
Common hurdles in addressing wildfire arson 19
What does serial wildfire arson look like? 22
Conclusion 25

3 Investigation co-operation and collaboration **27**

The collaborative investigation approach 28
Information sharing and analysis 31
Conclusion 36
Annexure A – Example of a basic Memorandum of Understanding (MOU) 37
Annexure B – Example of a Mutual Aid Agreement Standard Operating Procedures (SOPs) 41

4 Analysis of wildfire events **45**

Specialist roles 45
Information collation 47

The analysis process 50
What needs to be analysed? 51
Software programs 57
Conclusion 57

5 **Collaborative wildfire investigation tactics** 59

Confidentiality 60
Tactical options in the wildfire investigation incident action plan 61
Annexure C – Example of template of a Wildfire Investigation Incident Action Plan 71
Conclusion 72

6 **Community engagement** 73

Community engagement tactics 74
Urban-interface area strategy 75
Rural area strategy 76
General information sources 77
Conclusion 80

7 **Firefighter arson** 81

How big is the issue of wildfire firefighter arson? 82
Why do firefighters light wildfires? 84
Prevention policy and tactics 89
Investigating wildfire firefighter arsonists 93
Conclusion 99

8 **Training** 101

What training is applicable? 102
First response crews 102
Fire scene investigators 103
Wildfire investigation team members 105
Who else can benefit from this specialist training? 107

9 **Conclusion** 109

Index 111

Foreword

Many parts of the world are at risk of wildfires (also known as bushfires and forest fires). From North America to South Africa, Europe and Australia, many countries are well known to have suffered from devastating wildfire events over the years. However, with a changing climate, many other countries are now having to grapple with the challenge of wildfire risk, such as Asia, the United Kingdom and South America. What is clear is all countries at risk have to address the deliberate ignition of wildfires.

After a devastating wildfire season in 2009 in the State of Victoria in Australia, which resulted in the death of 173 people, thousands of structures destroyed and over 400,000 hectares impacted, the issue of wildfire arson emerged as a risk needing a national cohesive response.

The first 'National Forum to Reduce Deliberate Bushfires in Australia' was instigated at my initiative and held in March 2009, shortly after this major fire event. The aim of the Forum was to consider opportunities to share Bushfire Arson prevention initiatives and to identify national priorities for action through a 'National Action Plan for the Prevention of Bushfire Arson in Australia'.

Ten actions were articulated in the Work Plan; the first of which is to develop a 'National Strategy to Reduce Bushfire Arson'.

It was at this time I first met Superintendent Richard Woods, in his former role as Operations Manager with the Australian Capital Territory Rural Fire Service. Richard is uniquely placed to advise on these issues having had a long career in wildfire suppression and investigation, along with law enforcement in New South Wales (NSW). Richard was subsequently seconded to the Australian Attorney Generals' Department, to write the National Strategy and design initiatives to address this crime on a national level. He held briefings with me on a number of occasions and as part of the National Plan, adapted a multiagency training course he introduced from North America to Australia, designed to address the investigation of serial wildfire arson.

Over the next few years, I hosted a number of follow-up National Bushfire Arson Forums with Richard involved as Co-Chair of the National Bushfire Arson Prevention Working Group.

As part of his engagement, Richard also delivered additional 'Wildfire Arson Investigation Management' courses in 2011 and 2012 hosting police and fire investigators from across Australia, The Netherlands and New Zealand.

Richard's expertise in wildfire investigation and arson prevention makes him one of Australia's most highly regarded specialists in his field, travelling internationally to provide advice to fire and police agencies over the last few years.

This *Wildfire Arson Prevention Guide* is an essential reference for agencies around the world to address the risk of wildfire arson.

I applaud Richard's commitment in developing this comprehensive manual for international use. I am confident that it will provide practical strategies and tactics for law enforcement and fire agencies to address wildfire arson.

The Honourable Justice Robert McClelland
Deputy Chief Judge of the Federal Circuit and Family Court of Australia.
Former and Minister for Emergency Management and Attorney-General of the Commonwealth of Australia

Acknowledgements

Valerie Ingham, Associate Professor of Emergency Management, Charles Sturt University, NSW, Australia.

Mr. Jeff Henricks, Senior Investigator, Provincial Wildfire Prevention Officer, (ret.), Alberta Agriculture and Forestry, Canada.

Mr. Ken Ness, Detective Sergeant (ret.), Investigations Unit, Saskatchewan Ministry of Environment, Canada.

Mr. Paul Steensland, United States Forest Service Law Enforcement and Investigations, Senior Special Agent, (ret.), Oregon, USA.

National Wildfire Coordinating Group, Wildland Fire Investigation Subcommittee, Boise, Idaho, USA.

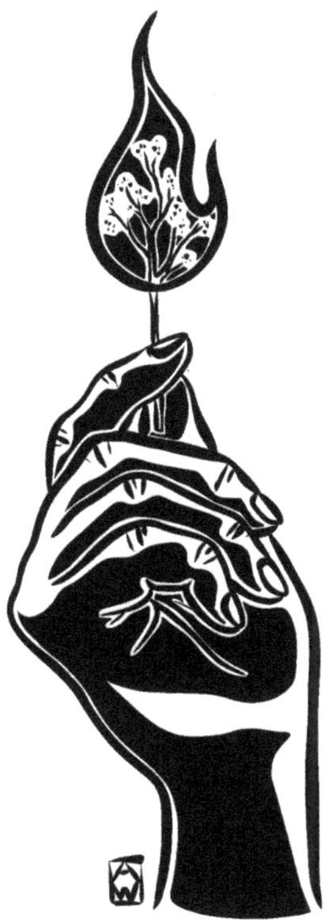

Illustration by Alexandra Woods.

About the author

I commenced my interest in wildfires in Australia with the NSW Rural Fire Service in 1976. I also served as a Police Officer in this State and later worked in frontline management in the New South Wales (NSW) and Australian Capital Territory (ACT) Rural Fire Services in south-eastern Australia over a period of 39 years.

In 2001, I established the Fire Investigation capability with the NSW Rural Fire Service and managed that role for 9 years, undertaking international study tours to the United States, introducing their latest wildfire investigation training packages to NSW to increase their investigation capability.

In 2009, as Operations Manager for the ACT Rural Fire Service, I instigated the introduction of the North American–based Wildland Fire Investigation Case Development Course to Australia, after modifying it for local use, delivering three courses to Australian and international students.

In 2010, the Australian Federal Attorney-General's Department engaged me to develop National Bushfire Arson Prevention arrangements, while serving as Co-Chair of the Australian-based National Bushfire Arson Prevention Working Group, addressing Bushfire Arson Prevention initiatives at a Federal level.

I have held the role of Adjunct Lecturer in Wildfire Investigation with Charles Sturt University since 2012, delivering training to international students, as part of the Graduate Certificate in Fire Investigation.

Since 2010, I have been the Director of 'Wildfire Investigations and Analysis', an international wildfire investigation consultancy, providing advice and training in Australia, Europe, South-East Asia and North America.

In 2004, I was appointed as Chair of the International Association of Arson Investigators (IAAI) Wildland Fire Investigation Committee.

For over 20 years I have been an associate member of the North American–based National Wildfire Co-ordinating Group (NWCG) Wildland Fire Investigation Sub Committee.

In 2013, I was awarded the Australian Fire Service Medal for my commitment to wildfire investigation in Australia.

During my career, I have completed a Graduate Certificate and Diploma in Fire Investigation through Charles Sturt University, along with a Graduate

Certificate in Applied Management at the Australian Institute of Police Management.

After working in Law Enforcement, in Wildfire Management and specialising in wildfire investigation, I have written this guide to assist jurisdictions to address the international issue of wildfire arson to provide a safer environment for their communities.

Richard Woods AFSM
Grad Dip Fire Inv; Dip Govt Inv; Grad Cert Applied Mgt

Introduction

Wildfire arson is often viewed as an abhorrent and inexplicable crime, which has the potential to cause damage, destruction and loss. When it impacts a community, there is often an outcry from the public for authorities to immediately arrest the perpetrators and penalise to the full extent of the law. An understandable reaction given the trauma and terror uncontrolled wildfire can cause. Importantly, every wildfire has the potential for tragic and catastrophic consequences. There are few crimes that can be executed using a readily available 'weapon' such as an inexpensive cigarette lighter or box of matches, and if timed with heightened fire danger conditions, the offender can successfully cause significant disruption and destruction to a community. A single match can tie up emergency services for hours, days and even weeks. And the related safety risk to the community and first responders impacted by wildfire is well known. Additionally, the financial cost of the suppression of a single wildfire event can be significant. With the increasing encroachment of urbanisation on rural lands around the world, the expanding urban/wildland interface provides a greater opportunity for individuals to deliberately light wildfires to impact on these developing communities (Figure I.1).

Figure I.1 ACT Rural Fire Service (Photograph by the author).

DOI: 10.4324/9781003353843-1

Why is wildfire arson assumed to be difficult to address?

It needs to be recognised that all countries that have a risk of wildfire experience varying levels of wildfire arson. However, the extent of their arson activity is sometimes not fully appreciated as it may be hidden in inaccurate or incomplete wildfire cause records or through limited event data sharing opportunities between response agencies. Investigations are also blurred by either regulation or practice resulting from demarcation 'lines' of responsibility. There are also jurisdictions around the world where a deliberate decision is made to avoid the true extent of their arson problem by not putting an emphasis on investigating suspected human-caused fires. A series of wildfire ignitions across a jurisdiction may not all be arson-related, however, until a proactive approach is taken to accurately determine their cause and ultimately reduce the number of ignitions, communities will remain at heightened risk from unplanned wildfires.

Consequently, it is also often considered an impossible crime to solve due to a lack of understanding of where to start an investigation and a perceived lack of evidence. Fire agencies tend to focus on upgrading suppression resources in an attempt to protect the community and the responsibility of catching the offenders is often given to law enforcement, who may not be well resourced to deal with this specialist area of crime.

This guidebook will demonstrate strategies and tactics that can be applied to accurately identify the cause of wildfires and those who are responsible (Figure I.2).

Figure I.2 Wildfires are a recognised risk in the Netherlands during the summer months (Photograph by the author).

How big is the issue of wildfire arson?

Experience suggests that most wildfire ignitions are a consequence of human activity, and it is, perhaps, not surprising that the majority are ignited in the urban/wildland interface. Most of these fires are small and cause no damage to property and are classed as 'low-risk' events. But often this is only due to mitigating circumstances such as the intervention of suppression crews, the fires are ignited during times of lower fire danger or the condition or availability of fuel, which is not conducive to extensive fire spread. However, these 'low-risk' events still pose safety risks to members of the public and first responders, such as the heightened risk to the fire crew and road users as fire vehicles respond to the incident using lights and sirens. Plus, these repeat fire events result in the ongoing use of wildfire suppression resources seeing an increase in operational costs to the agency.

It is important to recognise that the timing of wildfire ignitions is dependent on the natural cycles which influence heightened wildfire risk, such as the increasing flammability condition of wildfire fuel, weather factors and the resulting spike in the Fire Danger Index. The missing component is for an offender to provide an ignition source.

Dr. Colleen Bryant, as part of her study at the Australian Institute of Criminology in Australia in 2008, found deliberate wildfire ignitions are often seen as unplanned, often occurring close to populated areas and infrastructure. She also confirms these actions waste emergency service resources, place an additional cost burden on the taxpayer and the ability of emergency services to respond to other life-threatening events. She also found repeated fire events are detrimental to the environment in fire-sensitive flora changes contributing to species loss and changes in ecosystem biodiversity (Bryant 2008, p. 5).

Similarly in Europe, a study in Belgium saw patterns of human-related caused wildfires having impacts on biodiversity, "Our study also revealed that most wildfire ignitions in Belgium are caused by humans (both arson and negligence) and that natural causes such as lightning are rather scarce" (Depicker et al. 2020, p. 363). Whilst Belgium is not considered a country with a high wildfire risk, the area impacted is proportionate to the country's land mass. "The annual burnt area rarely exceeds 40 ha, but depending on the meteorological conditions relatively large areas – in a Belgian context – can be affected. Unfortunately, these fires often occur in biologically valuable nature areas" (Depicker et al. 2020, p. 370).

A similar study that reviewed fire causes across the broader area of Europe also found most fires were the result of human activity, "Overall, when all regions are considered together, it is observed that 97.1% of fires in Europe are directly or indirectly caused by human agents" (Ganteaume et al.

Figure I.3 Deliberately lit wildfires can cause significant risk to life and property as in this wildfire near Sydney, Australia (Photograph by the author).

2013, p. 652). This study also found arson featured in countries around the Mediterranean (Ganteaume et al. 2013, p. 651). In the United States, the National Parks Service cites the National Interagency Fire Center findings from 2000 to 2017, where the majority of wildfires in that country are caused by humans, "Nearly 85% of wildland fires in the United States are caused by humans. Human-caused fires result from campfires left unattended, the burning of debris, equipment use and malfunctions, negligently discarded cigarettes and intentional acts of arson" (NPS 2022).

Therefore, if not addressed, the issue of wildfire arson can pose significant risks to communities, countries and even continents, resulting in devastating impacts on their populations and the environment (Figure I.3).

Intent of this guidebook

The content of this guidebook is designed to give agencies options to address the problem of deliberately lit wildfire ignitions and provide strategies to solve the problem. It is intended to assist local fire, law enforcement and land management agencies within an area (state, county, shire, borough, region or province), where a pattern of recurring wildfires are occurring with unknown or suspicious circumstances relating to the cause of wildfires. Importantly, it recognises the need for collaborative investigations not only within jurisdictions but also across borders. Experience has seen some informal working relationships work in these circumstances, but the need to formalise arrangements is vital to ensure cross-agency support, particularly in complex or prolonged serial case investigations. Not all the content may be applicable to certain jurisdictions, but it provides optional strategies and tactics to be selectively applied to suit local arrangements. It is also recognised that some jurisdictions may have limited resources and skillset challenges to address the issue of serial wildfire arson activity. To this end, it recommends specialist training opportunities to improve the skillsets of agency personnel to address this crime. The use of the recommended strategies and tactics may not suit all jurisdictions due to the limitations of the powers and responsibilities of key agencies working within local legislation. It is therefore recommended that specialist legal advice be sought prior to implementing the strategies in this text. For example, the National Fire Protection Association (NFPA) suggests in relation to fire investigation data collection, "The investigator may need legal advice to properly gain access to certain types of data" (NFPA 2021, par. 14.2). Nevertheless, many of the operational recommendations within this text can be modified to suit local arrangements.

The ultimate aim of this text is to reduce the number of deliberately lit wildfires, provide ideas to help identify those responsible and result in a safer community.

References

Bryant, C. (2008). *Deliberately Lit Vegetation Fires in Australia. Trends & Issues in Crime and Criminal Justice No. 350*. Australian Institute of Criminology, Canberra, Australia. Viewed 1 November 2021, https://www.aic.gov.au/publications/tandi/tandi350.

Depicker, A., De Baets, B., and Baetens, J.M. (2020). *Wildfire ignition probability in Belgium*. Ghent University, Ghent, Belgium.

Ganteaume, A., Camia, A., Jappiot, M., San-Miguel-Ayanz, J., Long-Fournel, M. & Lampin, C. (2013). *A Review of the Main Driving Factors of Forest Fire Ignition over Europe*. Environmental Management Springer Science + Business Media, New York, NY, USA.

National Fire Protection Association (2021). *NFPA 921 Guide for Fire and Explosions Investigations*. Quincy, MA, USA.

National Parks Service (2022). *Wildfire Causes and Evaluations*, viewed 19 March 2022, https://www.nps.gov/articles/wildfire-causes-and-evaluation.htm#:~:text=Nearly%2085%20percent*%20of%20wildland,and%20intentional%20acts%20of%20arson.

Recognised wildfire arson motives

1

NSWRFS (Photo taken by the author).

The classification of the various 'types' of arsonist is defined by the National Wildfire Coordinating Group (NWCG) as,

> Single arsonist – an offender who sets a single fire then ceases. Spree arsonist- an offender who sets fires at three or more separate locations with no emotional cooling-off period in between the fires. Serial arsonist – a person who sets three or more fires, at the same or different locations, with an emotional cooling-off period between the incidents. The cooling-off period is the result of temporary psychological relief that results from the act of setting the fires.
>
> *(NWCG 2016, p. 313)*

In any wildfire at risk community, the hazard of these traits of deliberate fire lighting needs to be detected.

When a deliberately lit wildfire does occur and the community is impacted by a wildfire, these questions are asked: "Why did someone light this? What were they thinking?" Often naively, it is assumed that the person responsible must be a 'pyromaniac' or 'mentally deranged'. However, research suggests the reasons why people light fires, which are more complex and varied. Details outlined in the *Crime Classification Manual*, Douglas

DOI: 10.4324/9781003353843-2

et al. (2006), consider offenders' characteristics and their criminal acts in regard to their motivation. The first edition of this text was developed with the assistance of the US FBI National Centre for the Analysis of Violent Crime. It lists **six** arson-related motives namely,

- vandalism;
- revenge;
- excitement;
- profit;
- crime concealment and
- extremism.

(Douglas et al. 2006, p. 263)

It is also recognised that subsets align to these motives. For example, within the revenge category, individual, societal, institutional and group motives can be identified; within the excitement category, subsets of thrill and attention seekers or those seeking recognition can be found. Profit is importantly identified in the area of fire suppression contractors, who may benefit financially in providing a suppression capability to wildfire events. It has been said, "… the blacker the forest the greener the wallet!" (NWCG 2016, p. 310).

Two other models derived from research in Australia have similar motive descriptors. Debra Bennett and Michael Davis detailed these in *The Psychology of Arson* by Doley et al. (2016), referring to the *Behavioural Facet Model* by Canter and Fritzon (1998), which classifies arsonists based on their motivation and target.

These two orthogonal dimensions result in four behavioural themes;

- Instrumental-person (arson revenge against another person);
- Instrumental-object (arson committed to satisfy general criminal goals);
- Expressive-person (arson committed to obtain attention);
- Expressive-object (arson committed to provide emotional satisfaction).

> While these two typologies were developed in different ways there is obvious overlap between the various arson types.
>
> *(Bennett & Davis as cited in Doley et al. 2016, p. 192)*

A further model based on a study of serial arsonists who had committed at least three offences across *all* fire types in Australia, determined by Kocsis and Cooksey (2002), identified common themes of behaviour and showed a degree of planning; often, evidence was left at the fire scene, along with a relationship between the victims and the offenders. They also confirmed four specific sub-themes:

- thrill – fire lighting activity not related to any particular animosity involving high risk and sporadic attacks, which may be sophisticated and premeditated on unrelated targets, usually vegetation (interestingly, it is suggested that this does not involve any animosity compared with the following patterns);
- anger – fire lighting targeting residential properties or vehicles through a perceived relationship using fire to inflict harm;
- wanton – fire lighting through generalised animosity on unfocussed and vague targets (more likely to be structures of schools, universities and businesses) and
- sexual – fire lighting having a link to sexual excitement (most fires are small and target properties such as rubbish bins, post boxes and restrooms).

(Bennett & Davis as cited in Doley et al. 2016, p. 140)

This finding by Kocsis and Cooksey needs to be considered in the motives of arsonists that occur around motor vehicles and structure fires, having a divergent alignment to wildfire arson, based on a broader target context and opportunity.

The United States Fire Administration on page 6 of the 2003 Technical Report cites that 'firefighter arson' also refers to the same six primary motives behind serial fire lighting within this specific group of offenders as outlined earlier in the *Crime Classification Manual* by Douglas et al., (excitement, vandalism, revenge, crime concealment and extremist/terrorism and profit). This agency also highlights that those motives may change depending on the offenders' circumstances.

> Motives for arson, like other aspects of human behaviors, often defy structured, unbending definition. Strictly speaking, who can argue that vandals are not looking for excitement when they are engaging in their malicious mischief? Add an element of power and revenge and one can see the problem of strict, unyielding classification. …Be aware that motivations may change….
>
> *(US Fire Administration 2003, p. 10)*

The element of power through lighting of wildfires is recognised as an underlying theme across all motives, which is evident in research conducted by Tim Huff, a former analyst at the National Center for the Analysis of Violent Crime, FBI Academy of Wildfire Arsonists in the United States (Figure 1.1).

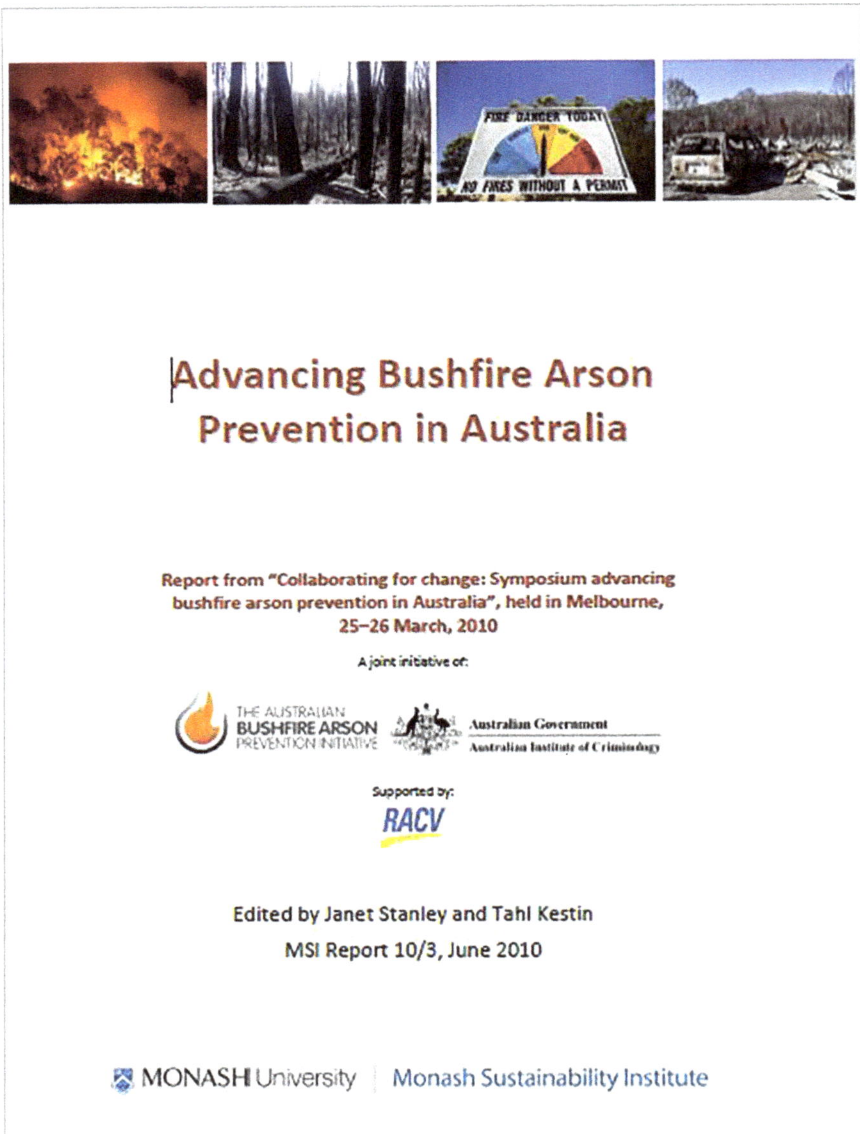

Figure 1.1 In 2010, in Australia, the author presented 'Advancing Bushfire Arson Prevention Forum' (retrieved from https://apo.org.au/sites/default/files/resource-files/2010-06/apo-nid21608.pdf). These events, such as this one hosted by Monash University Melbourne, Australia, are valuable to expand the understanding of the issue to key stakeholders.

It is important here to note that the opportunity to successfully ignite a wildfire is dependent on the fuel and weather conditions, whereas a structure or vehicle fire can be ignited at any time. Wildfire arsonists seeking to satisfy their motive of excitement by lighting a wildfire may be inspired to commit their act after learning of a weather forecast of hot and windy conditions, along with public warnings of a heightened Fire Danger Rating, thus creating an ideal opportunity for their ignition to result in a significant fire. This is in contrast to structure fire arsonists who can time their ignition without having to consider the influence of the weather and the availability of flammable 'fuel'. 'Experienced' wildfire arsonists may also time the lighting of their fire to avoid these dangerous conditions if they only intend to have their wildfire pose a limited size and a limited impact on the community. This is often the case in the behaviour of firefighter arsonists who may have the benefit of wildfire behaviour training to target their ignitions when the Fire Danger Rating is lower and the risk to surrounding property and life is reduced.

Commonalities of behavioural motive models

It is clear that all these motive models do have common linkages across all fire-type categories. These examples of models should be viewed as being in general context for profiling purposes, but what is apparent is both are seen to have a number of similarities, as depicted in Figure 1.2.

The investigation and subsequent laying of charges against an offender for serial wildfire arson do not strictly require a need to identify the motive behind the deliberate fire lighting; however, this aspect can be useful to assist in the early stages of an investigation to help narrow down who may be responsible in a community and may assist in predicting future targeted ignitions. The offender's motive may also be very valuable to include in the facts presented in a prosecution case. Importantly, it is recognised that most fire investigators generally do not have access to clinical expertise to assess the motive behind serial fire lighting. Seeking the skills of a criminal profiler may offer investigators some additional leads in their case and may be useful when limited background information is available to the team in the early stages of a case. For example, the identification of a financial motive could be the driver of deliberate fire lighting by an offender, and as such, it may provide leads to focus the investigation on firefighting contractors or on-call firefighters who benefit financially in support of fire suppression roles, particularly during the time of economic downturn in a community. This driver has been seen in Europe,

> Socio-economic factors such as the unemployment rate are increasingly taken into account when analysing fire causes in Mediterranean-type countries,

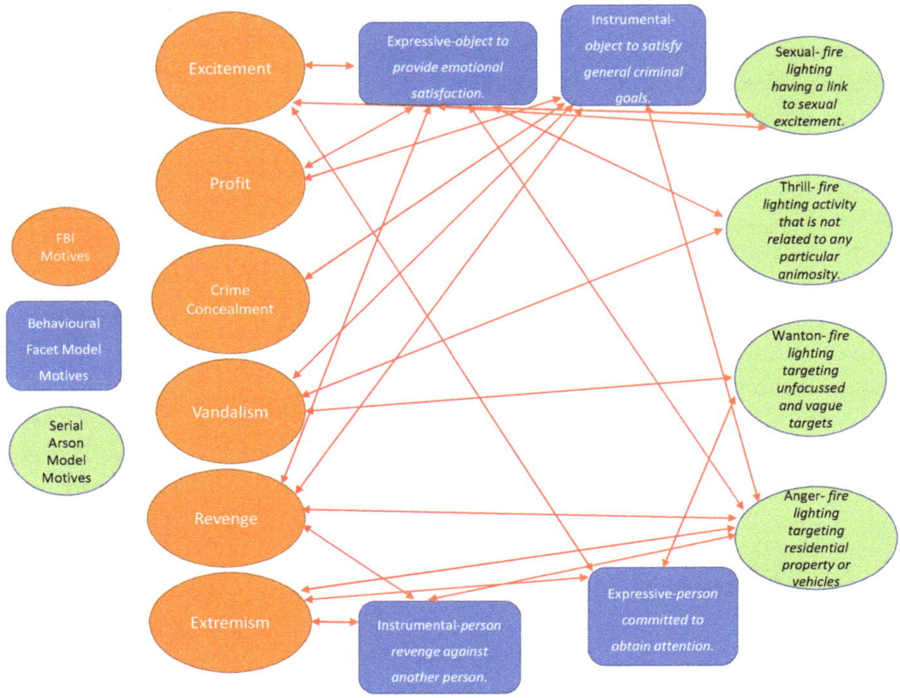

Figure 1.2 Similarities between motive theory models.

> as this factor has very often been linked with fire ignition. Indeed, several authors have pointed out that economic difficulties may promote conflicts that may result in the increase of intentional fires, which can be used as an instrument to force or maintain employment for seasonal workers (Bertrand & Baird 1975; Leone & Vita 1982; Ferreira de Almeida & Vilacae-Moura 1992; Leone 1999; Velez 2000; Martınez and others 2009; Lovreglio and others 2010).
>
> *(Ganteaume et al. 2013, p. 658)*

Nevertheless, it also needs to be acknowledged that varying conclusions were found across different communities when considering this motive. In a study in the United States, it was found that in some communities, there was not any increase in wildfire arson during economic downturns. Maingi and Henry (2007) found no relationship between the fire occurrence and county-level unemployment rate, whereas Prestemon and Butry (2005) showed that arson fires and economic factors such as poverty were related (Ganteaume et al. 2013, p. 658). Further research in this country did, however, find the opposite applied in some jurisdictions, "…locations with difficult economic conditions have higher rates of wildland arson, other variables held constant" (Prestemon & Butry 2005, p. 768). Importantly, this same study also suggested in response to this motive, "Given this, another strategy by law enforcement would be to pay attention to wildland arson in times of economic downturns and in places with chronically low wages and high poverty" (Prestemon & Butry 2005, p. 768). Therefore, to assist in identifying the persons responsible, it is important that investigators consider any relationship of serial arson to possible financial motives linked to local economic circumstances when conducting their investigations.

A further study in northwest Spain (an area rated as having one of the highest wildfire risk areas in Europe) showed that most fires in this region are caused by humans; however, an overestimate of deliberate fire lighting over misuse by the agriculture industry was a greater risk. Misconceptions were found in this study concerning 'pyromaniacs' being responsible for wildfires in this region: "The incidence of fires caused by pyromaniacs is often overestimated, not just by the general population but even by fire reporters and officials, due to the poor understanding of this mental disorder…" (Calviño-Cancela & Cañizo-Novelle 2018, p. 12). (The use of this term intermating a mental disorder in an offender is very much discouraged by experienced investigators and researchers). This finding underscores the need for agencies to more accurately determine the cause of wildfires in their area to ensure that a focus can be undertaken by a collaborative ignition prevention strategy. The Spanish study further clarified the actions of these individuals.

> Pyromaniacs engage in intentional and pathological fire setting, while arsonists willfully and maliciously set fire (or aid in setting fire). The highest probability of re-offending is in the first two years, and recidivist fire setters are likely to have mental disorders (Ducat, McEwan & Ogloff 2015 and references therein).
>
> *(Calviño-Cancela & Cañizo-Novelle 2018, p. 12)*

In contrast, research in Australia by Criminal Psychologist Dr. Rebecca Doley concluded after studying 140 incarcerated wildfire arsonists that, "Somewhat startingly, of the 39 offenders who admitted to serial arson, less than half (18; 46%) reported they had been convicted of any fire-related offence at some time in their criminal history" (Doley 2009, p. 91). This research confirms the limited rate of identification, arrest and conviction of wildfire arsonists in the past in a highly wildfire-prone country such as Australia. Likely, this trend would also be replicated in other countries where limited wildfire investigation expertise exists (Figure 1.3).

Figure 1.3 To conceal their crime, satisfy their general criminal goals and possibly in an anger response, offenders burn their previously stolen motor vehicles in forested areas, a significant issue in the cause of wildfires in many countries, as shown in this image. Shutterstock image.

Conclusion

Understanding the motive of wildfire arsonists is useful in identifying the offenders responsible, but not critical. It may give the investigation team areas to focus their intelligence analysis; however, experience has shown that some serial wildfire arsonists are convicted without any clear motive emerging. What is evident is investigators addressing wildfire arson require training and experience to gain confidence in addressing this unique and specialist area of investigation. Having this understanding, they can more effectively identify and address prevention measures within their jurisdiction. Once they are equipped to do so, these local circumstances need to be assessed to identify possible triggers that may instigate the serial wildfire arsonist to start their pattern of fire lighting, to lead to their arrest and may also add value to supporting a prosecution case at trial.

> Good knowledge of the causes of forest fire, of the related motivations and of the spatial-temporal distribution of fires is crucial for the design of prevention policies adapted tothe socio-economic, cultural and environmental circumstances of each region.
>
> *(Ganteaume et al. 2013, p. 658)*

References

Calviño-Cancela, M. & Cañizo-Novelle, N. (2018). Human dimensions of wildfires in NW Spain: causes, value of the burned vegetation and administrative measures. *Environmental Science*. Viewed 25 March 2021, https://peerj.com/articles/5657/.

Canter, D. & Fritzon, K. (1998). Differentiating arsonists: A model of firesetting actions and characteristics. *Legal and Criminological Psychology*, (Vol. 3), (pp. 73–96). DOI:10.1111/j.2044-8333.1998.tb00352.x.

Doley, R.M. (2009). *A Snapshot of Serial Arson in Australia*. Lap Lambert Academic Publishing, Saarbrucken, Germany.

Doley, R.M, Dickens, G.L. & Gannon, T.A. (2016). *The Psychology of Arson*. Routledge, Oxon, UK.

Douglas, J.E., Burgess, A.W., & Ressler, R.K. (2006). *Crime Classification Manual* (2nd edition). Jossey-Bass, San Francisco, CA, USA.

Ganteaume, A., Camia, A., Jappiot, M., San-Miguel-Ayanz, J., Long-Fournel, M. & Lampin, C. (2013) *A Review of the Main Driving Factors of Forest Fire Ignition Over Europe*. Environmental Management Springer Science + Business Media, New York, USA.

Kocsis, R. N. & Cooksey, R. W. (2002). Criminal psychological profiling of serial arson crimes. *International Journal of Offender Therapy and Comparative Criminology*, (Vol. 46), (pp. 631–656). DOI: 10.1177/0306624X02238159.

National Wildfire Co-ordinating Group (2016). *Guide to Wildland Fire Origin and Cause Determination*. Boise, ID, USA.

Prestemon, J.P. & Butry, D.T. (2005). Time to burn: modelling wildland arson as an autoregressive crime function. *American Journal of Agricultural Economics*, (Vol. 87)(3), (pp. 756–770). American Agricultural Economics Association, Hanover, PA, USA.

Stanley, J. & Kestin, T., eds. (2010). *Advancing Bushfire Arson Prevention in Australia: Report from a National Symposium, 25–26 March 2010*. MSI Report 10/3. Monash Sustainability Institute, Melbourne, Australia. Viewed 25 March 2021, https://apo.org.au/sites/default/files/resource-files/2010-06/apo-nid21608.pdf.

US Fire Administration (2003). *Special Report; Firefighter Arson*. United States Fire Administration, Federal Emergency Management Agency, Emmitsburg, MD, USA.

The wildfire arson investigation challenge 2

Wildfire resulting from two separate Ignition Areas (Photo taken by the author).

Experience shows that in many jurisdictions, wildfire arsonists carry out their work in communities knowing their past actions of lighting wildfires have gone undetected and as such, their confidence increases. Often, this behaviour can build over days, weeks, months or years. Like any crime, the more often an offender sees their wrongdoing going undetected, the more confident they become in continuing their behaviour in the absence of any deterrent effect. This is due, in part, to agencies missing the key signs of a serial arsonist at work. Many 'benign' fires that do not have any significant loss consequences are not investigated or are reported as accidental ignitions not worthy of any serious investigation. Consequently, the true causes of the wildfire series are 'buried'. But eventually, the day arrives when conditions come together with a heightened Fire Danger Index and the offender strategically sites the ignition that rapidly intensifies to cause a firestorm resulting in damage and destruction. Media coverage then focusses on the terrorised residents and asks, 'What is the cause?', which often results in senior agency officers pressuring investigators to expedite an investigation into the single devastating event. However, it was likely that a pattern of fire lighting was already occurring leading up to this disaster. Often, valuable evidence is

DOI: 10.4324/9781003353843-3

available to investigators to help identify the offender at the previous series of 'benign' wildfires that occurred across the area in the past.

The 'hidden problem' of the extent of wildfire arson

Similar to the opportunity to commit any crime, wildfire arson occurs because an opportunity arises – all that is needed is a motivated offender, a suitable target and the absence of capable guardians or a deterrence. And wildfire arson continues if there is a lack of awareness through limited education of the community (and agency personnel), of the importance of wildfire ignition prevention; if inadequate legislation is available to actively prosecute offenders or if there is not a consistent approach to wildfire investigation and law enforcement. This is represented in the 'Wildfire Ignition Prevention Pie' in Figure 2.1. If any one of these components is missing, the problem of human-caused fires will continue. Each one involves a strategic and tactical approach.

'Education' around the risks of wildfire arson. The community needs to be educated about the risk of wildfire arson and how it can assist in reporting suspicious activity around deliberately lit wildfires. It also involves educating agency personnel (first responders, agency chiefs and supervisors, prosecutors and even the judiciary) to emphasise the costs and risks that all unplanned wildfires cause, and importantly, train first responders in the accurate reporting of wildfire cause, along with their role in the information and evidence gathering process. This also includes the need to train firefighters in identifying wildfire causes as a key area of the education component.

'Engineering', through legislation, investigation protocols and resourcing, to ensure that key agencies have wildfire investigation capabilities, reporting and regulations in place. Sufficient numbers of trained investigators, along with required investigation equipment, underpinned by legislation and interagency agreements, are written to validate each agency's role within the jurisdiction to address the prevention, investigation and prosecution of human-caused wildfires.

'Enforcement', by providing a proactive investigation capability within a jurisdiction to investigate wildfire causes and to prosecute offenders. This component also acts as a deterrent to other would-be offenders in a community. Without a threat of prosecution, the arsonist has no fear of the consequences of being detected or prosecuted.

Agencies, therefore, need to address each of these areas through a range of strategic and tactical approaches in their jurisdiction, as a first step to addressing the issue of wildfire arson in their jurisdiction. Critical to the success of this model is the need to evaluate its success to ensure that the strategies and tactics of each component are effective or require modification.

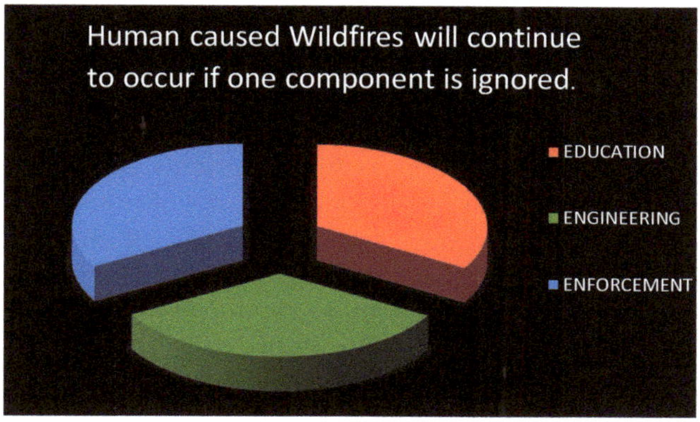

Figure 2.1 The Wildfire Ignition Prevention pie (Developed by the author).

Common hurdles in addressing wildfire arson

A secluded wildland setting can provide a suitable opportunity and 'target selection area' for wildfire arson. Planning is often undertaken by offenders to assess the level of risk of detection by witnesses, fire agency officers or law enforcement. Suitable weather and fuel conditions combined with a motive to light the wildfire is the last link in the chain for the arsonist to execute their actions.

These secluded wildfire arson target areas provide an ideal environment for the placement of a timed ignition device or a 'hot set', such as a single match with few or no witnesses, and as such, may be considered impossible to investigate. In many jurisdictions, experience shows that the fire agency attends and extinguishes the wildfire and deems the cause to be 'accidental' by a discarded cigarette (with no supporting evidence) or the circumstances around the cause to be 'suspicious' (again with no supporting evidence). The event is then referred to law enforcement (often untrained in wildfire cases) to investigate those who commonly already have high caseloads involving 'mainstream' crimes against individuals or property to solve, along with limited staff availability. These 'nuisance' wildfires that don't result in any property damage or injury if reported to the law enforcement agency often are only recorded as an event and are likely regarded more as a fire agency issue in the absence of any 'victim'. Unfortunately, fire agency managers may tend to view the extinguishment of these 'minor' wildfires as their prime role and as their firefighters successfully complete this task reporting no actual loss or damage. Or it is considered as 'pointless looking for evidence of an ignition source at a wildfire as there is never anything to find'. The fire service prepares for the next event, and the matter ends there. This approach is reinforced by the first responding fire crews having their role confirmed as confined to extinguishment and controlling of wildfires with any suspicious causes being the responsibility of law enforcement to investigate in isolation. Unfortunately, all too often under these circumstances, the true extent of the wildfire arson in the jurisdiction is consequently obscured.

In some jurisdictions, this approach is commonly also linked to the 'silo effect' of information and intelligence sharing, when the cause of these serial small and inconsequential wildfire events are passed off un-investigated and in some more remote rural jurisdictions un-reported. The reality is often the effort of accurately recording all wildfires, reporting the cause and finding patterns of ignition is the first step in solving these cases. But without any clear ownership of the problem of unplanned wildfire ignitions, nothing is achieved to prevent future wildfires – the offender continues to light wildfires undetected, often honing their skills resulting in more successful and significant events.

This silo effect of information exchange can be further compounded by jurisdictional boundaries. History has seen wildfire arsonists work across agencies, municipal/county or state boundaries undetected due to limited or no information sharing between agencies or jurisdictions. This can be further complicated as an arsonist moves residence between towns, regions or boroughs. A sudden spike in wildfire events in a jurisdiction may be a sign that an experienced offender has moved into an area after practising their skills in another jurisdiction, after a change in personal circumstances.

The main gaps in solving serial wildfire arson cases are also linked to a number of key factors. One critical flaw is not having data collated to conduct a pattern analysis or the linking of these events through basic analysis techniques (Figure 2.2).

Other missing links include the following:

- a failure to tie all associated events and compile key and easily obtainable information;
- a failure of investigators to extensively review cases and analyse them for patterns against fire history;
- a failure to cooperate across jurisdictional lines;
- a lack of or poor-quality fire scene examinations to identify evidence;
- a failure to manage all available information under a single case and
- not providing access to investigators from key participating agencies who have responsibility in preventing and investigating wildfires.

Generally, many of these missed opportunities are referred to as 'linkage blindness' arising from a lack of recognition to recognise common factors across wildfire events. A former Senior Special Agent with the US Forest

Figure 2.2 First attending fire crews questioning a 'witness' at a wildfire scene in Guam, Mariana Islands. Often, arsonists will return to the scene to view the response of the fire service and the resulting fire damage (Photograph taken by the author).

Service found in his experience in investigating wildfires over his career, linkage blindness was the result of common oversights.

> The reasons for this included: fires being set in different jurisdictions, failure of the upward reporting system, lack of emphasis on thorough scene investigations of "nuisance" fires, fires being investigated by different personnel, fires being investigated by unqualified personnel, a lack of awareness of pattern analysis and other linking techniques, organizational impediments to internal and external communication and a failure to accurately identify arson as the cause.
>
> *(Steensland n.d., p. 44)*

The complex and extensive nature of wildfire investigation data requires a capable case management system to readily identify trends.

As in the case of all crimes, wildfire arson will often occur when three conditions are met as outlined in Figure 2.3:

- motivated offenders;
- opportunity (vegetated areas where fuel and weather conditions are conducive to successful wildfire ignition and spread) and
- lack of capable guardians to deter the offender (such as fire agency patrols, wildfire arson prevention programmes, community education officers, parents, police and teachers).

Figure 2.3 Crime Triangle (Clarke & Esk cited in Christensen 2007/08)

Socio-economic factors that are already mentioned can sometimes be a trigger for wildfire arsonists. What is clear is the correlation between certain population densities and the rate of wildfire arson, which can then be influenced by these socio-economic factors. Investigators may be able to anticipate the likelihood of wildfire arson activity if they can interpret some of these trigger points by instigating measures to actively focus investigations on deterring similar events of wildfire arson within the same community.

What does serial wildfire arson look like?

Serial arson is defined as, "Repetitive firesetting, sometimes called serial fire setting or serial arson, refers to a series of three or more (incendiary) fires, where the ignition is attributed to the individual or a group acting together" (NFPA 2021, par. 23.4.2). When considering serial wildfire arson, it is often flagged after a series of a more significant number of events than identified by the NFPA, as many are initially misreported as 'accidental' cause such as 'cigarette' or 'unknown'. Notwithstanding, the alert to the presence of serial arson should be flagged in analysing the number of wildfires in a particular zone as being *above what would be expected across the area of response.* Comparing wildfire event numbers to adjoining or similar jurisdictional areas may give the first sign that arsonist activity is heightened in an area. This was the experience in an Australian study reviewing wildfire events,

> Deliberate fire hot spots are characterised by high rates of fires per person, and commonly account for a high proportion of fires in a region, and potentially in a state or territory. High fire concentrations are evident across all agencies with responsibilities in the vicinity of the hot spot, so a genuine picture of the incendiary activity can only be achieved by combining data from each of the relevant agencies.
>
> *(Nicolopoulos cited in Bryant 2008, p. 1)*

The primary land use in the area can also influence the location and number of deliberate wildfire ignitions. For instance, forest management activities,

> Sometimes, management exacerbates the risk of wildland arson, while other actions alleviate the risk. Although our statistical finding that timber harvesting activity is a positive risk factor is not proved to be causal, these results are consistent with other research (Prestemon et al.).
>
> *(Prestemon & Butry 2005, p. 768)*

Agencies must be aware of the need to monitor shifting locations targeted for successful ignitions as a direct consequence arising from changes in fuel availability or forest management activities, such as the removal of available fuel after prescribed burning activities. These trends should be compared against adjoining jurisdictions to review the frequency and location of wildfire ignitions across a broader area.

The 'routine activity theory' according to Clarke and Eck (2003) (as cited by Christensen, 2007/2008, p. 695) (otherwise known as the 'Crime Triangle'), as depicted in Figure 2.3, links an individual's opportunity to committing a crime by taking advantage of local circumstances. Put simply in the wildfire arson context, arsonists have a motive to light a wildfire; they have available suitable forested area, which has fuel loads and conditions vulnerable to a successful wildfire ignition and an awareness that they can undertake the offence with little chance of being detected or prosecuted. This model can shift as circumstances change, as arsonists gain confidence and may see ignitions target more populated areas such as roadsides; or in response to changes in forest management activities or a shift in land use due to expanding urban development, giving arsonists easier access to formally inaccessible forested areas (Figure 2.4).

It can also apply as a motivated offender moves into these areas where a lack of suitable guardians is in place (e.g. extended response times of law enforcement or fire department resources and limited opportunity to monitor new housing subdivisions as agency resources are not increased to proactively patrol these new areas of wildland–urban interface). In California, this risk is increasing as urban areas are expanding, creating an opportunity for wildfire arson. The need for agencies to monitor these expanding developed areas is also recognised as increasing the risk, resulting in changes in ignition trends.

> Massive areas of wildland vegetation have been developed and fragmented in California over the course of the 20th century (Hammer et al. 2007; Syphard et al. 2017), and the resulting extent and fragmentation of fuel surely has affected ignition trends and area burned. It may therefore be important to

Figure 2.4 Once ignited, a wildfire subject to a heightened fire danger rating can rapidly exceed the capability of the fire agency to successfully suppress it. Wildfire in Crookwell, NSW, Australia (Photograph taken by the author).

> monitor areas that are becoming newly developed, as these may be the most fire-prone areas on the landscape, with sufficient people to start fires and wildland vegetation to carry fires (Radeloff et al. 2018).
>
> *(Keeley & Syphard 2018, p. 796)*

The higher risk target areas for arsonists are also confirmed in a study in wildfire-prone Mediterranean countries, where it was found that the majority of ignitions occur close to agricultural or urban areas. This study went on to find,

> In southern Italy, for instance, Lovreglio and others (2010) identified as major motivations of voluntary fires those linked to policies concerning seasonal forest workers; in this case fires were used as an instrument to force or maintain seasonal employment. In Galicia (NW Spain) and in northern Portugal, arson is also a major problem and has its roots in social conflicts around land use issues. In some cases, the conflicts arose because government plantations were established on lands that were previously used as rangelands by the local community (Moreira and others 2001; Tabara and others 2003).
>
> *(Ganteaume et al. 2013, p. 654)*

What this research confirms is that the opportunity for wildfire arson also can be related to unique circumstances affecting a community. Agencies must, therefore, be aware of the range of these local influences that may trigger wildfire arson in their jurisdiction to gain a thorough appreciation of the size of the problem they face, which may also allow for more targeted prevention strategies.

Conclusion

The challenge in identifying the extent of the wildfire arson problem in an area is often hindered by a lack of appreciation of triggers such as socio-economic, political and other local issues that may be driving the rate of wildfire arson. A lack of witnesses, use of delay incendiary devices, lack of scene investigations and poor data collection, along with a misunderstanding of the options available to investigate serial arson, leads the confusion about where to start to address this crime. Ultimately, like any crime, to solve serial wildfire arson there is a need to collect accurate and timely information through committed and appropriately resourced investigators working in a cross-agency investigation team. This approach with a commitment from the top of agencies to the frontline officers is necessary to ensure investigations are supported, information is gathered and co-operation between agencies will result in the successful identification of a serial wildfire arsonist.

> Serial arsonists often create a climate of fear in entire communities. Community leaders tend to compound the problem by pressuring law enforcement agencies to identify and quickly apprehend the fire setter. Often the arsonist evades apprehension for months as investigators become increasingly frustrated by a lack of experience in handling these baffling cases.
>
> *(Douglas et al. 2006, p. 289)*

References

Bryant, C. (2008). *Deliberately Lit Vegetation Fires in Australia. Trends & Issues in Crime and Criminal Justice No. 350.* Australian Institute of Criminology, Canberra, Australia. Viewed 1 November 2021, https://www.aic.gov.au/publications/tandi/tandi350.

Clarke, R. V. and Eck, J. (2003). *Become a Problem Solving Crime Analyst In 55 Small Steps*, Jill Dando Institute of Crime Science, University College London, London.

Christensen, W. (2007/08). The Prevention of Bushfire Arson through Target Hardening. *Flinders Journal of Law Reform*. Department of Natural Resources & Water, Queensland, Australia.

Douglas, J.E., Burgess, A.W. & Ressler, R.K. (2006). *Crime Classification Manual* (2nd edition). Jossey-Bass, San Francisco, CA, USA.

Ganteaume, A., Camia, A., Jappiot, M., San-Miguel-Ayanz, J., Long-Fournel, M. & Lampin, C. (2013) *A Review of the Main Driving Factors of Forest Fire Ignition Over Europe*. Environmental Management Springer Science + Business Media, New York, USA.

Keeley, J.E. & Syphard, A.D. (2018). Historical patterns of wildfire ignition sources in California Ecosystems. *International Journal of Wildland Fire*, (Vol. 27), (pp. 781–799). Clayton South, VIC, Australia.

National Fire Protection Association (2021). *NFPA 921 Guide for Fire and Explosions Investigations*. Quincy, MA. USA.

Prestemon, J.P. & Butry, D.T. (2005). Time to burn: modelling wildland arson as an autoregressive crime function. *American Journal of Agricultural Economics*, 87(3) (pp. 756–770). American Agricultural Economics Association, Hanover, PA, USA.

Steensland, P. (n.d.). *Serial Wildland Arson Analysis*. [Unpublished manuscript]. Grants Pass, OR, USA.

3 Investigation co-operation and collaboration

FI-310 Wildland Fire Investigation Case Development Training Course in Australia (Image by Wayne (Ham) Hamilton, New Zealand).

Experience suggests that wildfire arsonists do not recognise organisational or legislated boundaries, conducting their fire lighting where they are confident they will not be detected, most often in areas with which they are familiar. The location of jurisdictional or operational boundaries is common, not of any consequence to where the arsonist's target areas are located. An experienced arsonist may even use these boundaries to their advantage if they are aware of them *(e.g. firefighter arsonists who deliberately target areas within their district of responsibility to ensure that they are responded to wildfires they light).*

These scattered ignition locations often result in an incomplete picture of the extent of the wildfire arson problem in a region, when they extend over an agency operational boundary, resulting in disjointed investigations of wildfire events. In many cases, these incidents can occur over months or even years, often without any linkage of investigations.

Ultimately, geographical or jurisdictional areas of responsibility should not be a barrier to the collation of fire event data and the investigation of patterns of serial wildfire arson. To address these 'invisible' barriers, cross-agency

DOI: 10.4324/9781003353843-4

co-operation is essential to ensure a full picture of the size of the wildfire ignition problem.

The collaborative investigation approach

'Wildfire Arson Prevention Committee'. The first step to achieve a collaborative working arrangement is to establish a Wildfire Arson Prevention Committee to underpin the basis of the cross-agency working arrangements, made up of key agency representatives, such as fire agencies, law enforcement, local government and land management, who are authorised to dedicate and direct investigation resources on behalf of their agency.

To ensure success, the Committee and their investigation teams must have the following:

- a thorough appreciation of the extent of the wildfire arson problem;
- authority and ability to easily share and access wildfire data around a framework of confidentiality;
- an overarching agreement and commitment from each agency's executive to address wildfire arson through documented joint arrangements and
- members of the Committee need to have the appropriate level of training.

Importantly, they need to be driven by a collective goal, for example, "to reduce deliberate fire lighting in the xxx Province by 30 June 20xx, through the application of Mutual Aid Agreement Standard Operating Procedures". Active involvement from all agencies considered to have a responsibility to reduce wildfire arson must occur, such as local Law Enforcement (including crime scene representatives); Land Management Agencies (Federal/State/Provincial Forest Service and/or Federal/State/Provincial Parks Service); Fire Services (operational officer or ideally, a wildfire investigation specialist), an agency data analyst, all assigned to break down the 'silo effect' of wildfire data exchange barriers, as depicted in Figure 3.1.

To support the Wildfire Arson Prevention Committee, doctrine needs to be adopted, confirming collaborative and co-operative arrangements are in place to address wildfire arson at strategic and tactical levels. These supporting documents underscore for all agency personnel, how agencies respond to manage wildfire ignitions, particularly when significant wildfires, serial or spree ignitions impact on an area.

The Committee's engagement should occur year-round, to maintain up-to-date data exchange and analysis to inform the proactive investigation of wildfires.

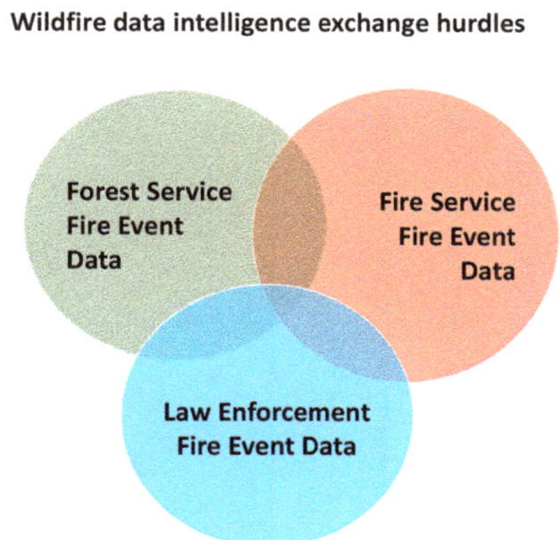

Figure 3.1 Wildfire event information 'silos' due to limited co-operation and investigation skills, impeding wildfire investigation collaboration and success. (Illustration developed by the author).

'Memorandum of Understanding' (MOU). The second step for the Committee is to establish an MOU approved by each executive officer from the Wildfire Arson Prevention Committee, to ensure that no jurisdictional hurdles are encountered across geographical and legislative boundaries. An example of key areas to consider in such an MOU is included in 'Annexure A'. This is a broad strategic agreement designed to address the general issues in the investigation of wildfires and detail a uniform approach to address the issue by the Committee.

MOUs are commonplace in many wildfire-prone jurisdictions of the world, when used to address mutual aid arrangements for sharing of resources during fire suppression or policing operations. To validate the role of the Wildfire Arson Prevention Committee, the MOU outlines the agreed arrangements to address wildfire arson across the agencies involved.

It needs to consider local arrangements and legislation and identify protocols, such as who will be involved in the investigations across each jurisdictional boundary, triggers for assistance or upscaling of an investigation, management of evidence and availability of specialist skillsets (Figure 3.2).

As a minimum, MOUs should include the following:

- introduction to detail the establishment of the co-operative arrangements;
- an organisational chart for the investigation teams based on the Incident Command System;
- a register of the agencies involved;
- a general statement of support addressing a collaborative approach to wildfire investigation;

Figure 3.2 The author examining a wildfire scene with law enforcement crime scene and uniformed police in Australia under Memorandum of Understanding protocols (ACT Rural Fire Service).

- a general statement agreeing to cross-agency protocols of media engagement specific to wildfire investigations;
- statement of agreement for financial support for cross-agency investigations and wildfire arson prevention;
- a reference to the implementation details on roles and responsibilities of each agency in wildfire investigation;
- a statement acknowledging the establishment of a 'Wildfire Arson Prevention Committee' and associated 'Wildfire Investigation Mutual Aid Agreement Standard Operating Procedures (MAA SOPs)';
- a statement to address the procedure in the event of cross-agency conflict within the MOU arrangements;
- a statement addressing the timing of the MOU termination and review;
- a statement of specific definitions relating to the jurisdiction and wildfire investigation arrangements and
- document approval by agency executive representatives.

MAA SOPs. The third step is to establish procedures in support of the MOU to govern tactical arrangements for investigation teams from each agency. This very focused document includes agreements on what information is shared, identification of key agency expertise to form investigation teams, how trend analysis data will be generated to identify wildfire ignition clusters, investigation activation protocols, including scene examination response as broadly outlined in Figure 3.3.

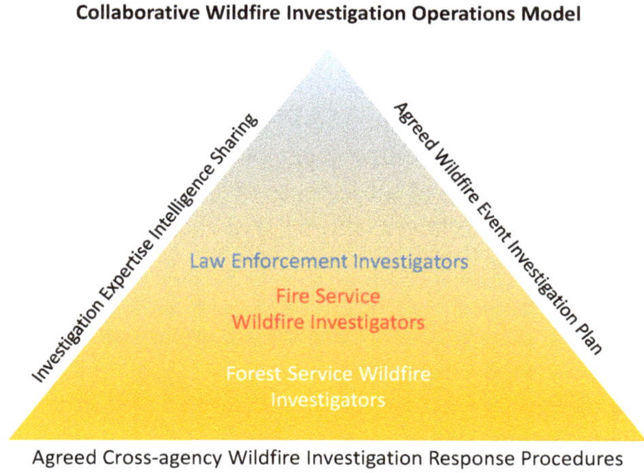

Figure 3.3 Collaborative Wildfire Investigation Operations Model (Illustration developed by the author).

The contents should cover practical aspects of collaboratively investigating wildfires under the auspices of the Wildfire Arson Prevention Committee. Based on the intent of the MOU, the MAA SOPs provide tactical details of how wildfires will be investigated and identify roles and responsibilities.

A key part of these MAA SOPs is the inclusion of other cross-agency-supporting tactics, such as community engagement initiatives to encourage information and intelligence gathering, as covered in greater detail in Chapter 6.

Information sharing and analysis

A key component of the MAA SOPs is to detail arrangements for the sharing of digital event information from each agency. Linked data platforms must be established before the onset of serial arson events. Unfortunately, often the building or integration of these databases can be technologically complex linking different systems used by agencies across a jurisdiction. The writing of digital data links is often a time-consuming technical project, requiring collaborative finances to assist with establishment costs from each agency, along with a 'host' organisation to maintain the system. What may appear to be a simple process of joining data fields can often require extensive planning and time-consuming work to achieve.

To ensure that all wildfire event data from each key agency are accessible and secure, an agreement on the central agency host needs to form the basis of the sharing process. This secure platform needs to be identified and managed by a lead agency. The establishment of a secure website is recommended by the NFPA in the United States. It states, "Websites are an efficient means of communicating information and can be constructed in a manner that limits access to the interested parties or may limit access to only certain areas of the website to certain interested parties" (NFPA 2021, par. 28.3.3). As such, this restricted access must form the first layer of security containing key information to allow the analysis of all aspects of the events. Experience shows that there are often many officers who believe that they are entitled to view investigation data; however, it needs to be closely managed to ensure only the key officers involved in the investigation team and their supervisors have this access. This is particularly important when an agency officer (e.g. firefighter) is at the centre of the arson investigation.

The desired capability of this common operating platform program is to link and share the following:

- historical and real-time wildfire event data including scene examination reports including fire scene evidence (Figure 3.4);
- reported persons of interest and their background information;
- witness versions of events;
- details of first attending crews;
- emergency service reporting line informant details;
- tip-line information (e.g. via Crime Stoppers);
- geospatial data to compare and contrast locations and fire-type identification of anchor points/exclusion areas/buffer zones and target areas;
- chronological assessment capability to compare the time of day and day of week/month and
- Assessment of reported cause; first attending crew report; geographical links of fires within a similar timeframe based on distance.

Ideally, the platform program must include live data feeds off response dispatch systems, to allow all key investigation representatives to have access to wildfire outbreaks in real time as they are reported, particularly on high fire danger index days.

Traditionally, agencies have been reluctant to share data due to confidentiality protocols within their departments. However, agreements between these agencies through the MOU must overcome any agency reluctance to share information and intelligence retained by key agencies in line with Figure 3.5.

The foundation of addressing collaborative and co-operative investigation arrangements between agency representatives is vital to overcome the 'silo-effect' of wildfire event intelligence and event data sharing as previously

Figure 3.4 Evidence (such as this footprint) at wildfire scenes can be valuable to link events and offenders to those events (Photograph taken by the author in Guam).

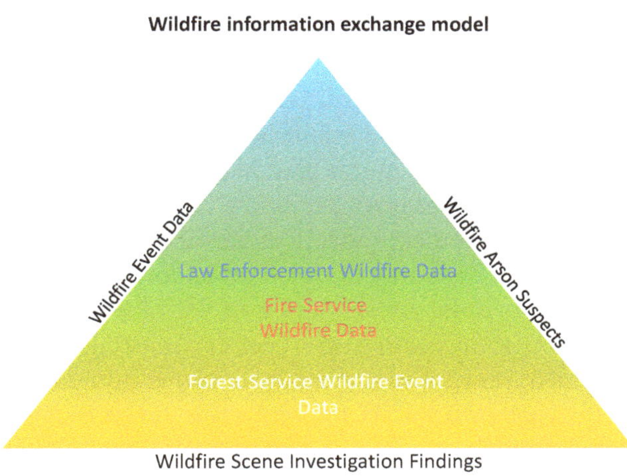

Figure 3.5 Wildfire information exchange model (Illustration developed by the author).

detailed in Figure 3.1. This is further complicated in jurisdictions involving numerous City/Municipal/County/State/Provincial/Federal boundaries. Sharing of key data will result in a greater level of co-operation and success in identification and prosecution of arsonists, making communities safer and reducing costs in emergency service response to wildfire ignitions.

In Australia, this collaborative approach was recognised in the findings of a Royal Commission, established after disastrous bushfires affected the State of Victoria in January 2009.

"...the Commission concluded that the main components of a successful community-based program for dealing with deliberate fire-setting and arson are likely to be as follows:

- ...an awareness of arson 'hot spots' in order to tailor interventions, reduce costs and potentially increase effectiveness
- use of intelligence to help guide prevention and detection activities
- high levels of co-operation with the community – including delivering a consistent message in a range of ways that is are tailored to the particular audience
- a coordinated response between the fire service and the police...."

(VBRC. Teague et al. 2010, p. 193)

The MAA SOPs should also include operational models that detail wildfire arson deterrence and detection strategies endorsed and resourced by key committee agency members. An Australian version of this approach is demonstrated in a rural-based collaboration plan, from the State of Victoria. The 'Gippsland Arson Prevention Program' (GAPP) includes Victorian law enforcement, fire agencies, local government, private and government forestry and power supply companies. The program deals not just with arson identification and prevention but also with accidental, negligent or carelessly caused fires including proactive coordinated fire prevention patrols by participating agencies across private and public lands, including an education program to deter arson. This procedural plan also links to state-level strategies and tactics as detailed in the State of Victoria's 'Operation Firesetter' strategy, which involves law enforcement patrols undertaking crime prevention and monitoring activities in high-risk bushfire arson locations during high-risk periods. It promotes mandatory activation of wildfire detection operations on extreme fire danger days before wildfires occur being made up of emergency management agencies and industries across a regional area. The GAPP approach may give agencies additional options to be considered as part of a jurisdictional SOP model.

As a priority, the MAA SOPs also detail tactical arrangements of when and how agency investigators will work together to investigate a fire scene, a series of fire scenes or the functionality of an ongoing investigation operation. It is acknowledged that these contents may not suit all jurisdictions. Nevertheless, the development of the MAA SOPs should be written to *overcome jurisdictional barriers* and not to become a reason why collaboration cannot occur. (An example of an outline of the contents of a basic MAA SOP is included in 'Annexure B').

'Wildfire Investigation Incident Action Plans'. The preparation of Wildfire Investigation Incident Action Plans may be required to respond to a series of serial wildfire ignitions or to investigate a major wildfire event. These are designed to address the agreed activation, response and operation of an investigation team (on a scalable basis) to reflect the extent of the wildfire ignition events emerging in an area. Draft templates of these plans should be prepared and refined prior to the onset of the fire season to detail specific tactics to focus on the investigation team's actions as wildfires occur. They are designed to include all aspects of the tactical considerations of a wildfire investigation including the goals of an investigation operation, organisation structure, taskings, response protocols, case reporting arrangements, investigation tactics, logistics and, importantly, investigator safety considerations. Notably, the identification and availability of other specialists that may be needed such as expert consultants should also be included.

They should be a concise 'living' document, specifically written to keep the investigation team focused on the wildfire series under investigation. They are valuable in managing prolonged investigations where the roles of team members change over time. (Further details are outlined in Chapter 5 and in 'Annexure C').

The example provided does not comprehensively consider the likely content of a Wildfire Investigation Incident Action Plan as it should be flexible and based on local arrangements and jurisdictional protocols, along with the likely scenario that may be regionally encountered in a serial wildfire arson case.

In summary, the relationship of the Wildfire Arson Prevention Committee to the MOU, MAA SOPs and Wildfire Investigation Incident Action Plans is represented in Figure 3.6. It should be seen as an integrated approach from each agency providing support and detail of how the collaborative arrangements operate across areas of responsibility.

Significantly, agency investigator authority limitations need to be considered at all levels when these documents are prepared to account for local legislative arrangements. Agency roles should complement the intent to remove identified 'gaps' that may inhibit the investigation roles, for example, ensuring team members the right of entry when investigating a fire scene on private property. To appropriately address the legality of these cross-agency arrangements, agency lawyers should be consulted to validate each prior to their enactment.

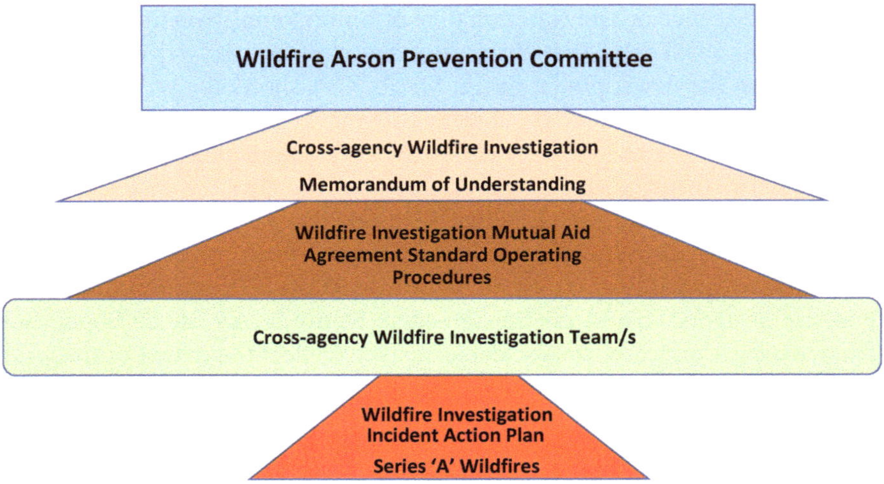

Figure 3.6 Relationship of the Wildfire Arson Prevention Committee, MOU, MAA SOPs and Wildfire Investigation Incident Action Plan (Illustration developed by the author).

Conclusion

The ability for an at-risk wildfire area (such as a county, shire, borough, state or province) to formally and successfully address the issue of wildfire arson is dependent on the co-operation and collaboration of agencies that share wildfire management and law enforcement. The harnessing of specialist investigators' skills under agreed protocols is crucial, along with their ability to work with their respective cross-agency endorsement and authority. All agencies can benefit from sharing resources and expertise. Experience shows that a formal and collaborative approach is necessary to ensure the best opportunity for success. The establishment of these protocols allows the investigation team to operate more confidently and successfully to identify and prosecute wildfire arsonists.

> Although a particular agency may have primacy of an investigation a collaborative team approach by all agencies is now seen as best practice.
>
> *(Victorian Fire Investigation Inter-Agency Agreement 2016, p. 4)*

Annexure A – Example of a basic Memorandum of Understanding (MOU)

WILDFIRE ARSON PREVENTION COMMITTEE

MEMORANDUM OF UNDERSTANDING

.... *(Jurisdictional area governing this MOU)*

(Insert Agency Logos here).

XXXX FOREST SERVICE
XXXX FIRE DEPARTMENT
XXXX POLICE DEPARTMENT

DATE OF APPROVAL;

WILDFIRE ARSON PREVENTION COMMITTEE MEMORANDUM OF UNDERSTANDING

1. INTRODUCTION

This Memorandum of Understanding (MOU) is intended to provide an overall framework for co-operation and joint operations involving the prevention of wildfire arson through the examination and investigation of wildfires within the xxx *(Jurisdictional area governing this MOU).*

This agreement recognises the operational jurisdictions and responsibilities of each service and their specific responsibilities under Legislation.

(Refer here to Legislation and specific powers and responsibilities to conduct Wildfire Investigations).

2. AGENCIES INVOLVED

2.1 Forest Service Roles and Responsibilities
2.2 Fire Department Roles and Responsibilities
2.3 Police Department Roles and Responsibilities

3. STATEMENT OF INTENT

3.1 *(A collaborative overarching statement outlining an aim to reduce wildfire arson events through joint arrangements within the jurisdiction, supported by the Mutual Aid Agreement SOPs).*

4. MEDIA ENGAGEMENT PROTOCOLS

(Arrangements for reporting of joint wildfire investigations by agency's senior officers).

5. FINANCE AGREEMENT FOR JOINT ACTIVITIES AND INVESTIGATIONS

6. IMPLEMENTATION AND REVIEW OF THIS MEMORANDUM OF UNDERSTANDING

7. ESTABLISHMENT AND RESPONSIBILITIES OF THE WILDFIRE ARSON PREVENTION COMMITTEE

8. CONFLICT RESOLUTION

9. TERMINATION AND REVIEW CRITERIA

10. DEFINITIONS

11. APPROVAL

Chief of Police	Chief of Fire Department	Chief of Forest Service
Name:	**Name:**	**Name:**
Date:	**Date:**	**Date:**

Annexure B – Example of a Mutual Aid Agreement Standard Operating Procedures (SOPs)

WILDFIRE INVESTIGATION MUTUAL AID AGREEMENT STANDARD OPERATING PROCEDURES

For use by Members of the 'xxx County/Shire/Region Wildfire Investigation Team'

(Insert Agency Logos here).

Review date:

Example Contents

Introduction
Wildfire Investigation Memorandum of Understanding *(reference to this document)*
SOP 1 First Attack Crew Awareness
SOP 2 Authorised Wildfire Investigators
SOP 3 Establishment and role of the xxx County/Shire/Region Wildfire Arson Prevention Committee
SOP 4 Basic Equipment for Wildfire Investigation
SOP 5 Standard Personal Protective Equipment for Wildfire Investigation
SOP 6 Response of Wildfire Investigation Teams
SOP 7 Scene Examination Protocols
SOP 8 Recording of Wildfire Investigations
SOP 9 Collection and Management of Evidence
SOP 10 Investigation Team Structure
SOP 11 Reporting of Investigations
SOP 12 Sharing of investigation intelligence and wildfire data
SOP 13 Wildfire Investigation Safety
SOP 14 Community Engagement Strategy

Introduction – *(a supporting statement of the agreement between the agencies to collaborate and co-operate in the investigation of wildfires).*

Wildfire Investigation Memorandum of Understanding *(A reference linking the relationship of the MOU to this document for a common approach to wildfire investigation tactical arrangements).*

Standard Operating Procedures.

SOP 1 First Attack Crew Awareness – *(content to highlight the need to train first responder crews to preserve wildfire scenes, identify evidence and report causes).*

SOP 2 Authorised Wildfire Investigators – *(content to detail the process of appointing qualified Wildfire Investigators on a common arrangement across participating agencies, including minimum standard qualifications, competency standards, training and minimum activity requirements).*

SOP 3 Establishment and role of the xxx County/Shire/Region Wildfire Arson Prevention Committee – *(outline of the agency membership representation, strategic functionality of the Committee and general functionality of information sharing and wildfire ignition prevention within the Committee, etc.)*

SOP 4 Basic Equipment for Wildfire Investigation – *(based on best practice, minimum standard for wildfire investigation equipment as recommended by the NWCG).*

SOP 5 Standard Personal Protective Equipment (PPE) for Wildfire Investigation – *(recommended minimum standard PPE for field scene examinations).*

SOP 6 Response of Wildfire Investigation Teams – *(details the notification and response arrangements to reported wildfire events by pre-determined investigation teams).*

SOP 7 Scene Examination Protocols – *(detail the arrangements for the response of the investigation team to examine wildfire scenes, scene security and legal right of access to private property).*

SOP 8 Recording of Wildfire Investigations – *(confirms standard reporting requirements across agencies, including image management, and cause analysis reporting).*

SOP 9 Collection and Management of Evidence – *(outlines roles and responsibilities in collecting, retaining and analysing evidence collected from the wildfire scene).*

SOP 10 Investigation Team Structure – *(detailing the roles, responsibilities and reporting lines of an integrated investigation team using the Incident Command System. Identification of suitably qualified and authorised investigation personnel from across key agencies to fill key roles of IC, PIO, Liaison, Planning and Operations – including reporting Investigation Team/s and Logistics, are identified to perform these roles prior to an investigation taking place).*

SOP 11 Reporting of Investigations – *(details how and where investigation information will be stored, secure data sharing/access arrangements and access authority).*

SOP 12 Sharing of investigation intelligence and wildfire data – *(details the agreement of what is shared, authorised access, where it is hosted, analysis support and review by team members).*

SOP 13 Wildfire Investigation Safety – *(details agreed on safety protocols across agencies while investigating wildfire scenes).*

SOP 14 Community Engagement Strategy – *(details core community education programs to raise awareness of the issues around wildfire arson).*

(These titles are examples only and jurisdictions should include SOPS to account for the joint working relationship considerations to be addressed).

References

National Fire Protection Association (2021). *NFPA 921 Guide for Fire and Explosions Investigations.* Quincy, MA, USA.

State of Victoria (2016). *Victorian Fire Investigation Inter-Agency Agreement.* Melbourne, VIC, Australia.

Teague, B., McLeod, R. & Pascoe, S. (2010). *2009 Victorian Bushfires Royal Commission: Final Report.* 2010 Victorian Government. Viewed 1 February 2022, http://royalcommission.vic.gov.au/Commission-Reports/Final-Report.html.

Analysis of wildfire events

4

FI-310 Wildland Fire Investigation Case Development Training Course in Australia (Image by Wayne 'Ham' Hamilton, New Zealand).

A common issue in trying to gain a picture of a serial wildfire arson problem is when incidents are not connected through limited or incomplete analysis processes. The size of the problem can be made clearer through a number of analytical steps and ideally, via the engagement of a qualified analyst to identify patterns and links across events. Identifying links around serial wildfire events can provide the investigation team with valuable information, "After patterns are detected in a serial arson case, much can be learned to help predict the next event and classify the behavioural patterns exhibited by the offender" (Icove & Haynes 2018, p. 692).

Specialist roles

The analysis of serial wildfire arson is often considered a critical area of an investigation, due to the complexity of the crime and variables that may affect

DOI: 10.4324/9781003353843-5

the successful ignition of wildfire fuel. To undertake these investigations successfully, all agency investigators should complete specialist training in serial wildfire investigation. The North American–based National Wildfire Co-ordinating Group (NWCG) 'FI-310 Wildland Fire Investigation Case Development Course', provides one of the few internationally deliverable training opportunities for investigators to obtain skills to learn the issues in analysing information and identifying serial wildfire arsonists. (Details on the content delivered are outlined in Chapter 8.) The flowing content is based primarily on the critical aspects of the theory within this training course.

Key agency members of the Wildfire Arson Prevention Committee should identify specialist staff they may make available to guide and assist investigation teams in the analysis of event data. This can often be a complex and significant workload particularly when an extensive number of wildfire events are to be analysed from different agency records.

To enhance the quality of fire cause determination findings, experienced wildfire scene examination experts need to be identified by the investigation team to examine fire scenes as new incidents occur and if necessary to revisit old fire scenes to gather information and revisit previous wildfire cause determinations. These officers must be trained in the NWCG 'FI-210 Wildland Fire Origin and Cause Determination Course' and be competent in the wildfire scene examinations (Figure 4.1).

As previously stated, the engagement of an experienced criminal analyst to provide advice on incident trends can ensure the key aspects of events to be considered to identify trends. Ideally, these officers should also have a background in the issues involved in serial wildfire arson. As most law enforcement

Figure 4.1 Author delivering wildfire investigation training in South Korea (Photograph taken by Veerachai Tanpipat, Thailand).

agencies will have access to these officers, it is appropriate that they can be approached to provide this resource as part of the investigation team.

In the absence of a criminal analyst, investigation team members can conduct a preliminary analysis of incident information using basic software tools to identify trends. Importantly, the accuracy of this analysis process is dependent on the quality of the information recorded in the past by first responder crews and wildfire investigators.

To complement this role, the engagement of a Geographic Information System (GIS) Specialist is another valuable addition to the investigation team. Their role is to provide accurate recordings of the locations of ignitions and items of evidence and, importantly, conduct assessments of fire locations using pattern analysis and geospatial profiling. These staff should also have the ability to conduct field surveys as part of fire scene examinations, recording dimensions of fire scenes and the location of key evidence. The roles are valuable to identifying the arsonist and are vital in the prosecution process.

Information collation

As mentioned, the wildfire scene examination team may need to revisit past wildfires that were not examined or were previously reported as 'undetermined' or 'accidental' causes, extending back over months or even years in the area of interest, for example, to re-examine nearby fires to attempt to verify their cause, months or years apart.

The ongoing timely and accurate identification of wildfire causes is a critical part of the analysis process. Therefore, evidence management practices and protocols need to be in place for the safe and timely management of fire scene evidence, which often can be managed through law enforcement team members (e.g. the identification and recovery of ignition device evidence at fire scenes can be vital to link offenders across fire events through identified modus operandi and signature ignition devices, along with potential recovery and analysis of DNA from an offender on this evidence) (Figure 4.2). This work can often be deemed laborious; however, without a methodical approach, the linkage of events can be missed – delaying or missing an opportunity to identify the arsonist.

The use of other specialists may also be of value, such as technical officers experienced in the field of digital tracking technology and covert surveillance, K-9 (ignitable liquid detection and tracking) teams and aviation observers, to bolster the information gathering process. The extent of resourcing is dependent on the scale of the events being investigated and should be managed in line with the recommended process outlined in the FI-310 training package.

Figure 4.2 The location and recovery of evidence of the ignition source is vital, such as the remnants of this match (Photograph taken by the author).

Jurisdictions may not be fully aware they have a problem of wildfire arson until a broad analysis of all wildfire event data (e.g. times, dates, locations, causes etc.) is undertaken to identify when events started to 'spike'. A process of examining past statistics in one or more five-year 'blocks' of wildfire events until a noticeable spike of the commencement of fire events can be detected.

To avoid the camouflaging of a jurisdiction's wildfire cause records, a proactive approach often needs to be adopted to investigate the cause of wildfires in line with limited expertise availability. As such, there is also a need to upskill officers at the first responder level to have them more accurately report on the cause of wildfires they attend and to be able to preserve the scene for examination, by training them in the 'NWCG FI-110 Wildland Fire Observations and Origin Scene Protection for First Responders' Course (detailed in Chapter 8).

The investigation team should adopt a triaged approach to identify when formal scene examinations must take place as the formal investigation of every wildfire event is not practical for most agencies. An agreed cross-agency response protocol should identify which wildfire events qualify for formal scene examinations. An example of this model is provided in Figure 4.3 designed to ensure that more consistent arrangements are in place to accurately determine and report the wildfire cause in an area.

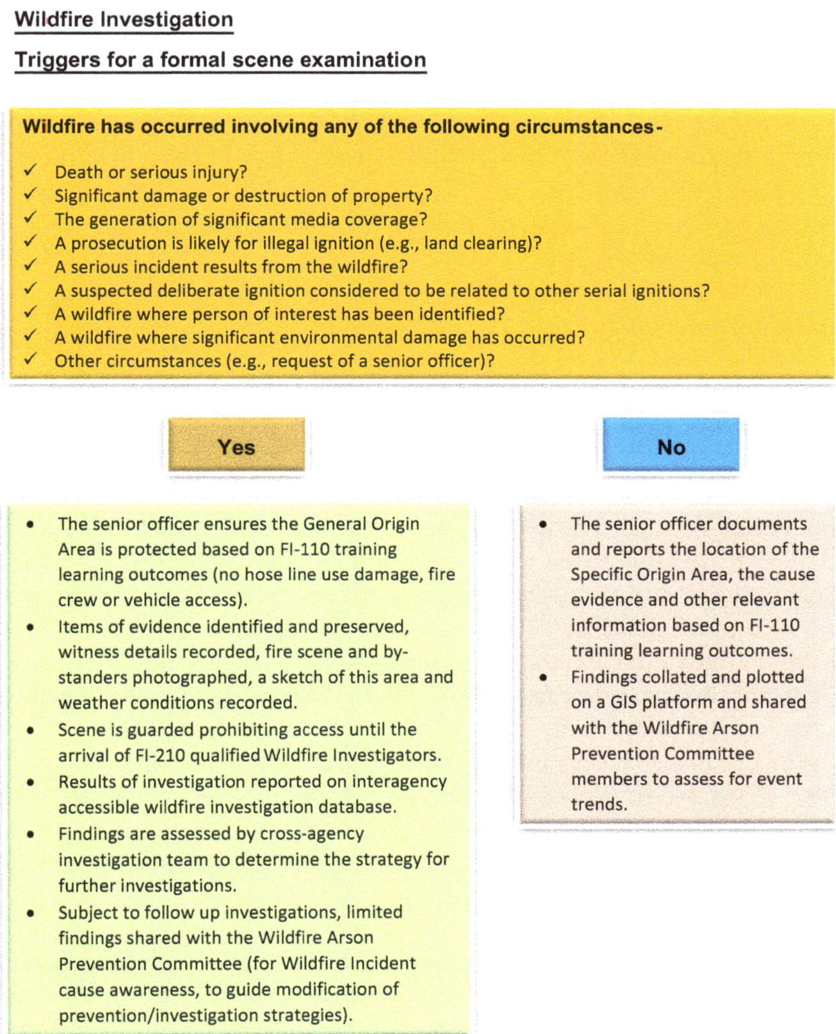

Figure 4.3 Example of trigger point flow diagram to assess if a formal wildfire scene investigation needs to take place (Illustration developed by the author).

This increased level of fire cause information can then form the basis of the analysis for future trend prediction modelling. This process involves the analysis of records of locations, dates and times of historical data to determine an 'out of the ordinary' change in the wildfire event occurrence for the area. And should this process not identify a significant decline in ignitions within a recent timeframe, further historical archived data must be reviewed. Any unaccounted dramatic decline or spike in ignitions, in the absence of obvious influences such as weather, identified through this process needs to become a focus point as an investigation strategy for the investigation team. For instance, this may see a need to review local circumstances that may provide a motive or opportunity to identify persons of interest who may be associated with the wildfires (e.g. those who may have moved into or out of the area, changes in economic circumstances or the transfer or hiring of fire suppression personnel).

The analysis process

To achieve successful investigation outcomes, it is vital that the circumstances of all fires need to be reviewed from different angles to identify any likely links. This requires a more vigilant approach from all involved from the first attending fire crew looking to accurately report their findings at the scene such as the suspected cause, evidence during the extinguishment process and witness information. A key foundation for successful investigations is to collate and share first responder and incident report records, which rely on cross-agency agreements.

Wildfire investigation information records that are shared need to be 'hosted' on a secure/closed database, accessible to select members of the investigation team. Team members such as the incident analyst can then access data based on specific area criteria to report trends over weeks, months and years. This is vital background work.

> The lack of a complete picture is likely to impact on how relevant agencies and government departments assess risk, the priorities that they assign to arson reduction and probably the effectiveness of the strategies that are introduced to mitigate risk.
>
> *(Bryant 2010, p. 1)*

As such, emerging trends may then be linked to local circumstances, as was found in a European Union study,

> In France, Alexandrian and Gouiran (1990) showed that intentional fires were mostly ignited in summer, towards the end of the afternoon or in the evening, while fires due to agricultural or forestry operations occurred more frequently in autumn-winter and during the day.
>
> *(Ganteaume et al. 2013, p. 656) (Figure 4.4)*

Figure 4.4 The proximity of the ignition of a wildfire to a roadway can be valuable to identify patterns of fire lighting, such as this early-stage wildfire in The Netherlands (Photograph taken by the author).

What needs to be analysed?

As would be the case in looking to link similar events in any crime category, the use of data needs to be compared across the jurisdiction and, if necessary, beyond it. There are four key areas to be analysed as recommended in the FI-310 training course:

- temporal data;
- geospatial data;
- target selection data and
- modus operandi/signature data.

1. **Temporal pattern analysis**

   This involves the comparison of the (likely) timing of wildfire ignitions to identify the trends in a given area through the analysis of all records analysing

   - times of the day when wildfires were reported;
   - days of the week when wildfires were reported and
   - days of the month when wildfires were reported.

   This analysis may reveal wildfire ignitions occurring on common times, days of the month or recurrent or non-recurrent clusters, which may suggest that the offender is available/not available to light fires. This area of analysis may also need to be compared with days when a particular Fire Danger Rating occurs. Trends may emerge that no wildfires are ignited in the region on days when the Fire Danger Rating exceeds 'Very High' or conversely, all ignitions align when 'Extreme' Fire Danger Rating impacts an area.

2. **Geospatial pattern analysis**

   This involves the comparison of the physical location of fires. It may reveal the following:

   - 'comfort zone' (as depicted in Figure 4.5), where offenders are familiar with the area and the activities in the area, tends to be

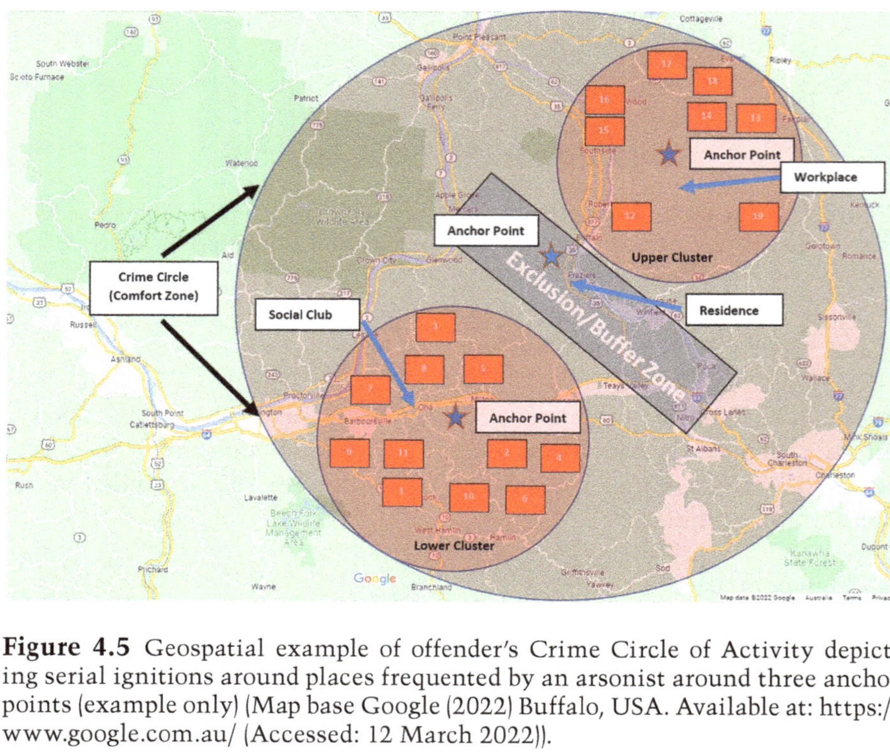

Figure 4.5 Geospatial example of offender's Crime Circle of Activity depicting serial ignitions around places frequented by an arsonist around three anchor points (example only) (Map base Google (2022) Buffalo, USA. Available at: https://www.google.com.au/ (Accessed: 12 March 2022)).

places frequented near their residence or workplace being anchor points. Offenders will commit the majority of their crimes within their comfort zone;

- 'crime circle' (where they are confident of lighting wildfires undetected) and
- 'pattern types' (circular expanding as depicted in Figure 4.6; circular imploding from the anchor point; linear expanding as depicted in Figure 4.7; linear imploding along roadways as depicted in Figure 4.8; multiple recurring repeat fires at the same location days, weeks, months or years apart from an anchor point as depicted in Figure 4.9; or a random/dispersed with no clear pattern from an anchor point).

Trends that may result from this analysis may identify the following features to identify where an arsonist may live, work or frequent.

3. **Distance decay**
   - The probability of igniting fires at a distance from the primary anchor points follows a decay function, that is, the further from home/work, the less likely there will be an offence.

Figure 4.6 Example of circular expanding pattern depicting the circular movement of ignition locations over time around an anchor point (example only) (Map base Google (2022) Harskamp, The Netherlands. Available at: https://www.google.com.au/ (Accessed: 12 March 2022)).

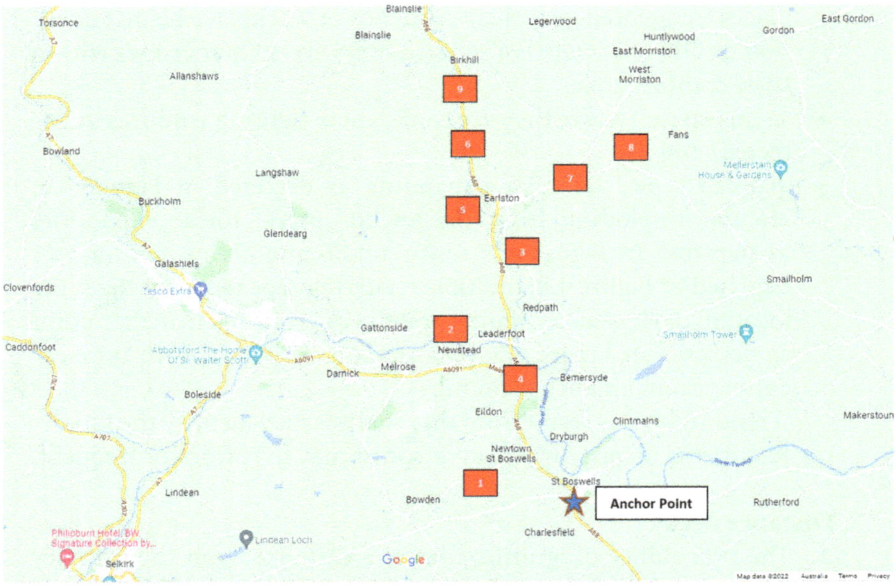

Figure 4.7 Example of linear expanding pattern depicting the linear movement of ignition locations over time from an anchor point (example only) (Map base Google (2022) Leaderfoot, UK. Available at: https://www.google.com.au/ (Accessed: 12 March 2022)).

4. **Buffer zone**
   - an area around the arsonist's residence, place of employment or other anchor points where no fires are set;
   - may be a relatively short or of a significant distance and
   - consciously selected to provide separation between critical areas where the arsonist frequents and their fires are set.

   Both are depicted in Figure 4.5 and Figure 4.9.

5. **Crime circle hypothesis**
   - a hypothesis that the arsonist's home or place of employment may be found within or adjacent to the perimeter of a crime circle;
   - the crime circle diameter is defined by the distance between the arsonist's furthermost fires.

   This is depicted in Figure 4.5.

6. **Primary activity areas** (upper cluster) are where the majority of offences occur. This is depicted in Figure 4.5.

Figure 4.8 Example of linear imploding pattern depicting the linear movement of ignition locations over time back to an anchor point (example only) (Map base Google (2022) Weddell, Australia. Available at: https://www.google.com.au/ (Accessed: 12 March 2022)).

Figure 4.9 Multiple Recurring depicting grouped ignition locations at differing times from an Anchor Point (example only). (Map base Google (2022) Guam, USA. Available at: https://www.google.com.au/ (Accessed: 12 March 2022)).

7. **Secondary activity areas** (lower cluster) are distinctly separate from the primary area.
   - often occurs towards the end of the series of arson actions, usually related to fear of apprehension and
   - overconfidence by the arsonist to ignite further wildfires.
   This is depicted in Figure 4.5.

8. **Exclusion zone** is where no fires are occurring between primary and secondary areas.
   Offenders may adopt the following five identifiable patterns:
   1. Circular
   2. Linear
   3. Multiple recurring
   4. Random/dispersed
   5. Travel route
   This is depicted in Figure 4.5.

9. **Target selection data**
   This evidence review considers the type of fuel/area the offender selects and links.
   - access/egress (e.g. walking trails with numerous access points);
   - risk of detection situations (e.g. roadside ignitions taking advantage of cover offered by bends or crests);
   - damage intent (e.g. targeting limited fuel load to inhibit fire progression or heavy fuel loading to ensure the maximum rate of spread and intensity);
   - fuel-type commonalities (e.g. always focusing on fully cured grassland fuel) and
   - victim targets (e.g. targeting national park land).
   This data linkage may provide a pattern of fire lighting that can be predicted in a geographical area to focus an investigation team response using covert surveillance options.

10. **Modus operandi data**
    This review analysis learned behaviour, such as how the wildfire was ignited (e.g. 'always uses a timed device using a cigarette bound with wooden matches'), recovered at repeated scenes through scene examinations.

11. **Signature analysis data**
    It considers unique details of the arsonists' actions that may be ritualistic or consistent but are not necessary to the successful ignition of the fire, for example, 'the construction of the

ignition device always uses four wooden matches with a specific brand of cigarette in the centre, fixed by a red rubber band'. This could include the arsonist leaving items at the scene not associated with the ignition.

Software programs

As previously mentioned, the use of an event software program is recommended to share and analyse information on wildfire events. Many law enforcement agencies have access to dedicated programs that analyse crime event data in their core role of policing. However, more recently, commercially available software designed to specifically analyse wildfire ignition events is becoming available, taking into account all the parameters as previously outlined. It has been the experience of the author using a version of the 'Extinguish Arson Intelligence Database' used by the Western Australia fire and police agencies. This system uses fire service data to link wildfire events, based on live or historical data of fire location and reported causes, along with time and date parameters. The software has the ability to marry informant information to identify ignition trends and give law enforcement team members access to also connect their intelligence information on their policing database. As is the case in this jurisdiction, arrangements should be an integrated software package that is also secure for use by dedicated wildfire investigation team members.

The actual review of ignition data needs to be carefully considered against the factors that influence the successful ignition of wildfires. For example, a study of arson trends in the United States acknowledged the hidden influence of weather in data reviews, "...arson ignition attempts could occur at a constant rate throughout a year, but it is only during certain weather that ignitions are successful. Lagged ignitions might then proxy for the unobservable local weather" (Prestemon & Butry 2005, p. 757). This confirms the need to have wildfire investigation expertise very actively involved in the analysis of data and the interpretation of results as in this finding, seasonal variabilities of successful wildfire ignitions based on weather and climate variations, limiting the flammability of fuels and limited wildfire spread.

Conclusion

A jurisdiction may be struggling with identifying an arsonist responsible for a spate of wildfire arson that appears to be random and unplanned. The key to solving these cases is to first gather accurate and timely wildfire event data and then comprehensively analyse it to identify common trends. This process provides a reliable means to focus an investigation and to inform the investigation team to drive the detail in the plan tactics.

> The temporal distribution of deliberate fires is consistent with routine activities theory (Cohen & Felson 1979), which states that a crime – in this case arson – takes place within the context of everyday patterns of movement and activity.
>
> *(Bryant 2010, p. 4)*

References

Bryant, C. (2008). *Deliberately Lit Vegetation Fires in Australia. Trends & Issues in Crime and Criminal Justice No. 350.* Australian Institute of Criminology, Canberra, Australia. Viewed 1 November 2021, https://www.aic.gov.au/publications/tandi/tandi350.

Ganteaume, A., Camia, A., Jappiot, M., San-Miguel-Ayanz, J., Long-Fournel, M. & Lampin, C. (2013). *A Review of the Main Driving Factors of Forest Fire Ignition over Europe*. Environmental Management Springer Science + Business Media, New York, NY, USA.

Icove, D. & Haynes, G. (2018). *Kirks Fire Investigation* (8th edition). Pearson, New York, NY, USA.

Prestemon, J.P. & Butry, D.T. (2005). Time to burn: modelling wildland arson as an autoregressive crime function. *American Journal of Agricultural Economics*, 87(3), (pp. 756–770). American Agricultural Economics Association, Hanover, PA, USA.

Collaborative wildfire investigation tactics

5

Capturing video evidence (Photo taken by the author).

The goal of every wildfire investigation is to determine where the fire was ignited, when it was ignited, what was ignited, what was used to ignite it and who is responsible.

It is important to recognise investigating serial wildfire arson events can often take extensive effort to gather all the intelligence and evidence necessary to achieve these goals. To an untrained investigator, this can be a daunting task. Additionally, experience often shows that wildfire cases prosecuted by inexperienced or untrained investigators are not successful when challenged through a legal process, due to lack of detailed evidence. Many of these cases could have been successfully prosecuted if the officers involved knew what critical evidence was required to prove the *case*.

This chapter outlines examples of tactics used in wildfire arson investigations, in line with those in the National Wildfire Co-ordinating Group (NWCG) 'FI-310 Wildland Fire Investigation Case Development Course'. The following provides examples of best practice tactics that can be employed in wildfire investigations, which can be included in MAA SOPs and Wildfire Investigation Incident Action Plans. As previously stated, to build the

DOI: 10.4324/9781003353843-6

investigation team's capability, it is strongly recommended that members of the investigation team undertake the full FI-310 training course to appreciate the application of proven tactics to ensure that they are applied where appropriate to solve this often-complex crime.

Confidentiality

The investigation team members must accept that they have the responsibility to maintain strict confidence in joint agency investigations. By its very nature, wildfire arson is targeted on the edge of suburbia in the urban interface or in rural communities, many of which have a close community 'network' of emergency service personnel responsible for the management of wildfire events, such as local volunteer fire departments and small municipal police departments. When conducting ongoing serial wildfire arson investigations in this context, the issue of confidentiality is often at risk through agency personnel being interested or observation of the investigators and their tactics. This has been seen as an important challenge in past investigations by experienced investigators in the United States, "Local officers or firefighters who become aware of a surveillance operation also pose a risk, as they may accidentally 'spill the beans' when bragging to someone in the area" (Nordskog 2013, p. 83). The investigation needs to spell out confidentiality protocols that are agreed to by the investigation team to ensure that their operations are not compromised through internal agency 'station chat'. The co-locating of the investigation team well away from local agency buildings or in an adjacent town is a practical measure to ensure the security of the investigation.

The investigation team also faces challenges in providing progress of the investigation to their respective chain of command. The related political reporting processes can also create another issue for individual agency investigators to manage, particularly during spree wildfire arson events that are capturing the interest of local media. These internal hierarchical reporting arrangements will see investigators having to manage the expectations of their respective executive officers 'right to know' of the progress of the investigation over the need to maintain strict confidentiality. While this is a normal reporting requirement in administrative matters, these reporting arrangements must be modified through the Wildfire Arson Prevention Committee MOU and MAA SOPs, well before the joint agency investigation team is activated. Experience has shown that cases have been compromised when this avenue of information flow is not strictly managed (Figure 5.1).

Figure 5.1 Wildfire burning during the 'Black Summer' fire season in Australia (Photograph taken by the author).

Tactical options in the wildfire investigation incident action plan

For some jurisdictions not experienced in the management of a complex wildfire investigation, the drafting of the Wildfire Investigation Incident Action Plan can be a challenging exercise. However, it is a valuable step to ensure that the goals, objectives and tactics of the investigation are clear to all members of the Wildfire Investigation Team. They also allow for the breakdown of key elements of the investigation along with identifying resource needs in line with the recommended adoption of an Incident Command System (ICS) structure, to clearly identify the investigation team members' roles and responsibilities. These elements are particularly important that investigators from different agencies are expected to work together, in some cases for the first time. The investigation team relies on the plan that needs to detail the agreed tactics to conduct the investigation, identifying specific roles and reporting responsibilities within the team.

The following outline the areas for consideration by the investigation team to include in a Wildfire Investigation Incident Action Plan. A template including an example of issues to be considered in a Wildfire Investigation Incident Action Plan is detailed in 'Annexure C'. *Aspects of these issues are provided below however, more comprehensive details on key tactics are delivered in the NWCG FI-310 Training Course.*

Safety – The safety of investigators is vitally important during wildfire investigations. Particular reference to investigators working in the field and the safety considerations need to be addressed specific to the area involved;

for instance, officers' safety (unarmed investigators, uniformed/non-uniformed officers), dealing with suspects or working in remote communities, team members working long hours during wildfire events, fireground safety considerations, remote area communications or mitigating risk when investigating fire agency personnel suspected of lighting wildfires. Specific tactics may need to be adopted to address the variable challenges of working in a remote rural area. For example, a tactic within the Wildfire Investigation Incident Action Plan that may be applied in monitoring an urban-interface Primary Activity Area in a remote rural setting having limited radio or mobile telephone coverage, or investigators working in small communities who may be hostile to government personnel. All areas that may impact the safety of investigators will need to be addressed in the Wildfire Investigation Incident Action Plan.

Scene examinations – Detailing the agreed response arrangements for the timely examination of wildfire scenes as incidents occur and which fires will be investigated across a geographical region, protocols for scene security and availability of specialist equipment to capture scene information. Similarly, who is the activation point of contact, what roles individual agency investigators will play in the scene examination process and how investigation report data are to be managed.

The scene examinations must be undertaken accurately in accordance with the recommended and accepted methodology in the investigation of wildfires. Importantly, it must be understood that structural fire investigation techniques do not apply to wildfire investigations due to the different ways wildfires and structure fires behave; wildfires being in an open environment exposed to influences of fuel, weather and topography, v's a confined environment of a structure, with fire progression heavily influenced by the design of a building. Therefore, it is essential that all wildfire investigators qualify in a specialist wildfire investigation training course such as the NWCG Wildland Fire Origin and Cause Determination Course (FI-210).

The key components are as follows:

Professional standards/investigator safety – Detailing the professional standards associated with this role and covering hazard awareness in wildfires. Working a post-forest fire scene can be hazardous, and investigator's safety is the highest priority.

Fire behaviour and fire pattern indicators – Critical to the process of investigating a wildfire scene. Provides a detailed understanding of wildfire behaviour and how the 11 categories of macro-scale and micro-scale fire pattern indicators are formed and can be interpreted. (These are further detailed in Chapter 8.)

Methodology – Application of the 'scientific method' in the investigation of wildfires and the process to be followed in examining a fire scene combining interpretation of fire pattern indicators and how to locate the General Origin Area, being, "The area of the fire that the wildland investigator can narrow down based on macroscale indicators, witness statements and the fire behaviour context. It may be a limited area or several acres in size but is typically less thann one half acre in size." (NWCG 2016, p. 119).

Then the task is to locate the Specific Origin Area, "The smaller area within the General Origin Area where the fire's direction of spread was first influenced by wind, fuel or slope" (NWCG 2016, p. 119) and then define the Ignition Area, "Contained within the Specific Origin Area will be the smallest location which a wildland fire investigator can define, within the Specific Origin Area, in which a heat source and fuel interacted with each other and a fire began" (NWCG 2016, p. 119). These areas are detailed in Figure 5.2. A sample of basic scene examination equipment items to identify these areas are detailed in Figure 5.3.

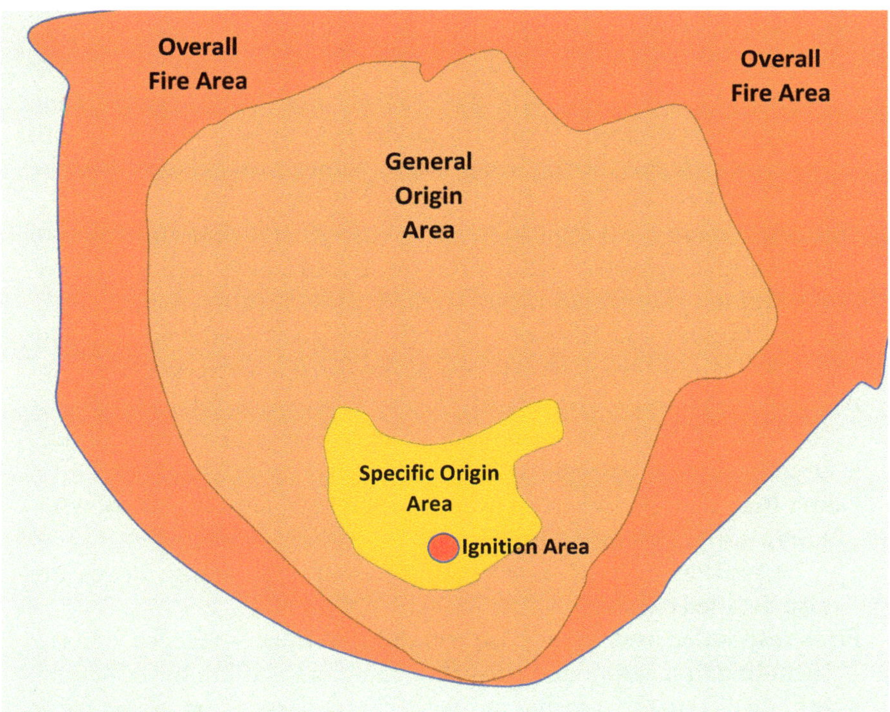

Figure 5.2 Parts of a wildfire scene examination (Illustration designed by the author).

Figure 5.3 Coloured flags/arrows form part of a scene examination kit used to mark fire pattern indicators to represent fire progression from the origin of a wildfire (Photograph taken by the author, Alberta, Canada).

Fire scene evidence – Provides detail on what physical evidence can be found at a wildfire scene and examples of techniques to recover this evidence to maintain a chain of custody for analysis and preservation.

Witness interviewing – Provides guidelines on how to speak with witnesses as part of the scene examination process in a wildfire investigation.

Documentation – An important part of the process of examination of a wildfire scene, which details recommended legally sufficient documentation to accurately record a wildfire investigation scene.

Ignition factors and sources – Details the recognised wildfire cause categories and the ignition processes involved in each cause.

Arson recognition – Importantly, this unit provides details of indicators of a wildfire arson event and the signs of typical ignition devices used by wildfire arsonists.

Court Preparation – gives an overview of typical legal aspects of wildfire investigation case management

(Associated scene examination-related supporting tactics are also detailed below).

First responder and agency information sources – Agency officers, including first responders, dispatch operators and fire tower observers, are vital to the information-gathering process. Suppression crews must be trained to observe evidence of fire cause and record information from witnesses to complement their role in the early stage of the wildfire. These crews are also in a strong position to identify and protect evidence at the scene of items that may relate to the fire cause and evidence of an arsonist at the scene. If not protected, these items can be destroyed in the suppression of the fire and not highlighted to the investigation team. As detailed in Chapter 8, the training of first responders is critical to ensure that they are aware of their role in the wildfire cause determination process (through the NWCG 'FI-110 Wildland Fire Observations and Origin Scene Protection for First Responders' Course) (Figure 5.4).

Additionally, access to agency in-vehicle/body-camera footage and firefighting aircraft video can provide high-value information. Dispatch Centre operators also play a key part, recording details on who reported the fire along with witness observations. Also, agency smoke spotter fire tower operators (now being replaced with remote camera technology) may capture the precise location of a fire in its initial stages and vehicles or people near the scene.

Neighbourhood/area canvas – Undertaking a canvass of people residing or working in the area of the wildfire ignition is an early step in the investigation and should be completed as soon as possible while witness's memories of the events leading up to and during the lighting of the wildfire. Often, valuable information can be obtained from this process along with access to local data records such as building security camera footage.

Documenting observers – Normally a function of the first responding crew, investigators who arrive on the scene of an active fire should

Figure 5.4 First attending firefighters at wildfire events are vital information sources for investigators. Wildfire in the Netherlands (Photograph taken by the author).

record details of members of the public watching the wildfire event, particularly vehicles being driven near the scene. The use of video or photographs can assist in this process.

Wildfire event analysis – Reviewing pattern analysis/geospatial profiling to ensure that any changes in wildfire ignitions are assessed against historical data. This is needed to ensure any ongoing ignitions are addressed by the investigation team and incorporated into the ongoing tactical response.

Wildfire K-9 teams – The engagement of specialist tracking teams to attend fire scenes as they are reported to trace the offender's movements from the scene and to accurately identify them. Note: A program using the bloodhound breed has been an outstanding success in the United States where the West Virginia Division of Forestry use trained wildfire investigators accompanied by bloodhounds to trace arsonists from the fire scene. The attendance of the bloodhound team is also a high-profile activity that can raise the awareness of the community of the investigation of the wildfire (Figure 5.5).

The use of ignitable liquid detection dogs specifically trained to work in a wildfire scene can also be of benefit to help locate the possible use of ignitable liquids as an ignition source, should there be an indication of its use.

Interviews – It is important to consider how the wildfire investigation team's expertise will be used at the various levels of the interview. The interviewing/canvassing of witnesses may be the role of trained

Figure 5.5 Bloodhound attached to the West Virginia Division of Forestry investigation team at a wildfire scene commencing tracking of an arsonist (Photograph taken by author).

members of the investigation team. However, given, it is often, that circumstantial evidence identifies a suspect, the interview of this person needs to be well planned and undertaken by an officer experienced in the investigation of wildfire cases. The interviewing officer must be well versed in the circumstances of the case and if considered necessary, he/she should be brought in from other law enforcement jurisdictions possessing interviewing expertise to interview the suspect.

In most instances, the interview of suspects needs to be supported by experienced wildfire investigators from partner investigation agencies. Other details of who will be involved in the formal interviewing of the offender and where will it take place need to be planned well in advance of an arrest.

Internationally, many wildfire investigators use the P.E.A.C.E model in undertaking interviews of witnesses and suspects involved in wildfire arson investigations.

This process involves the following:

P – Preparation and Planning establishing the interview 'environment' such as placement of the suspect at '10 to 2' position, in a quiet environment with adequate support to complete the interview such as documentation resources.

E – Engage and Explain the situation and the reasons for the interview to build rapport.

A – Account their knowledge of the event and the need to allow them to detail as much as possible through them reliving their experience. The first segment is free recalling of the events; the second is establishing focal points to identify and expand topics using *who, what when, where and how* questions. Then having the suspects recall events backwards to test the validity of what is being said, not using leading questions.

C – Closure of the process through verification from the suspect, if they have anything to add and the next stage in the investigation.

E – Evaluation by reviewing the information provided, its relationship to the investigation and evidence of offences and the urgency of further enquiries.

Physical evidence analysis – which officers will be assigned to manage the process of collection, storage and analysis of evidence.

Search warrants – which agency officers have the authority to execute and undertake property, person/s and vehicle searches. Importance to involve other members of the investigation team when conducting the search. Consideration of broad search for evidence, for example, suspect's workplaces, work vehicles and personal electronic items to be seized for analysis. Cases have emerged where the offenders have recorded images and videos on their smartphone of fires they have ignited as a personal record of their 'achievements'.

Open-source analysis – The analysis of social media channels by the investigation team can be a useful source of information providing a valuable avenue to identify offenders. Other considerations to check include online posts that may indicate links to wildfire arson for political purposes, such as terrorism.

Static surveillance via covert cameras – In field use of covert cameras on the entry and exit points of known clusters of wildfire arson activity can be of high value. This technology is often used by law enforcement agencies and has been critical in placing offenders in and around the scene of a wildfire ignition in arson cases. The cost and availability make them a very practical solution for extended monitoring of areas.

Technical/electronic surveillance – Real-time or intermittent movement monitoring of suspects using their mobile telephone or GPS tracker attached to their vehicle. It can be useful for extended monitoring timeframes, particularly during periods of low fire danger when suspects may cease their fire lighting activity until more favourable conditions for successful ignition return. Intermittent download options can provide a flexible/reduced investigation cost option.

Mobile surveillance – This tactic can be valuable if managed according to the setting, for example, in small communities and rural settings, as the ability of surveillance vehicles to blend into a small community and rural landscape can be particularly challenging and requires extensive staffing engagement. Therefore, it can be very problematic in the absence of electronic (GPS) surveillance monitoring of a suspect's vehicle.

License plate recognition cameras – The use of this technology can be proactively employed across areas where wildfire clusters are occurring. Linkage of vehicles of interest travelling in the area prior to and after wildfires are reported is valuable to the investigation to validate suspects' version of events and their movements.

Aerial surveillance – The use of aircraft or unmanned aerial vehicles to monitor suspects and their movements. Also, valuable to monitor known wildfire arson clusters during periods of predicted fire lighting activity or during high-risk days of heightened fire danger.

High-profile patrols – Fire, land management and law enforcement personnel can provide an excellent deterrent through the monitoring of known wildfire arson clusters when the risk to the community is too great during days of heightened fire danger, "Agencies could preposition law enforcement resources in locations where recent suspected wildland arson ignitions have occurred. They could also regularly increase arson enforcement on days and months of the year when ignitions are more common and during droughts" (Prestemon & Butry 2005, p. 767).

Crime Stoppers information – Encouragement of public assistance in obtaining witness information (sometimes anonymously). It can be of value in smaller communities where anonymity may provide an incentive to disclose information to the investigation team. Encouraged through the media and via the use of signage at the wildfire scene after the event, inviting the public to provide information on the circumstances of the wildfire ignition and the offender/s responsible. It can result in extensive amounts of information being provided, which requires the need for follow-up.

Media engagement – The engagement of the media can assist greatly by alerting the public to the ongoing investigation and inviting witnesses to come forward with information regarding the cause to assist the investigation team. Often, media outlets are interested to work with investigators, particularly after a community has been impacted by a serious wildfire suspected of being deliberately lit. They should also be advised of the conviction of arsonists through media releases and media conferences, involving representatives of the agencies engaged in the investigation. This also provides an opportunity to emphasise the formal wildfire investigation collaboration arrangements in place across agencies in the jurisdiction.

Informants – The use of financial incentives to provide information on the arsonist can work in some communities in the absence of investigation leads or validate event information.

Use of polygraph testing – Some jurisdictions may have this option via law enforcement agency investigators and can provide useful information when trying to narrow down wildfire arson suspects. Local arrangements will address the legality and procedures around its use. These key tactics provide some options to be considered by the investigation team for inclusion in the Wildfire Investigation Incident Action Plan. The use of other tactics should be included based on local circumstances and legislation. Land managers, fire service investigators and local law enforcement officers within the investigation team, are often in a strong position to have input into generating the best tactics for an investigation plan based as they often can use their local knowledge of the landscape and the community they serve.

The ability to adopt specific tactics involved in a serial wildfire investigation operation without being detected by a community is very challenging. This has been the experience of the author and other investigators when conducting investigations in at-risk wildfire communities. For example, when considering the use of covert surveillance cameras,

> People in rural areas are keenly aware of the hazards posed by arsonists, armed marijuana growers, thieves, and poachers, and they are often quick to spot any unusual activity – including undercover cops installing items along the road. Placing these cameras and recovering the data without being noticed is a skill that takes some learning.
>
> *(Nordskog 2013, p. 82)*

Therefore, the Wildfire Investigation Incident Action Plan needs to take into account all aspects of risk that may jeopardise officer safety and the exposure to community members of details of the investigation itself, by incorporating specific measures to address these risks.

Importantly, research and experience suggest that the adoption of at least three or more of these tactics is likely to successfully identify the arsonist, "In those cases where the suspect was apprehended as a result of a proactive investigative strategy, (rather than by chance), a combination of three or more of the identified tactics, applied concurrently, consistently produced successful resolution" (Steensland n.d., p. 3).

Annexure C – Example of template of a Wildfire Investigation Incident Action Plan

Xxxx REGION WILDFIRE INVESTIGATION IAP

Commencement date; xx xx xx

Review date; xx xx xx

Issue – Outlines the problem of wildfire arson being investigated.

Objective – States the goal of the investigation.

Investigation sensitivity – High-Confidential.

Agency representatives – Details the agency represented in the investigation team.

Organisational – Details lead roles across the ICS investigation team structure.

Division and sectors – Details specific roles of each area e.g. wildfire scene examiners, law enforcement crime scene officers, detectives, surveillance etc.

Communications – Details the team radio/mobile telephone communications arrangements.

Organisational reporting structure – Identifies the ICS roles across the investigation team.

Meetings/briefings – Investigation briefing procedures against the investigation objectives.

Investigation tactics – Based on the components as listed in this chapter as applicable to conduct the investigation. Updated as the investigation progresses.

The makeup of all tactics within the plan is fully flexible and should articulate collaboratively to best achieve a successful outcome involving key wildfire investigation expertise from across the jurisdiction.

Conclusion

The operational arrangements governing a wildfire investigation team need to meet the goal of the investigation and be workable within jurisdictional arrangements. The process of developing the investigation tactics should be undertaken on a team basis to ensure agency members' needs are addressed and a collaborative approach is achieved. This is particularly important when investigations can extend over a lengthy period.

> A model arson task force would incorporate the intelligence-gathering networks of each separate investigative agency into one cohesive, coordinated, and goal-directed entity...The sharing of investigative specialties (fire, police, e.t.c.,) and experience in a spirit of free-flowing communication would broaden the investigative capabilities of each investigator.
>
> *(O'Connor 1993, p. 4)*

References

National Wildfire Co-ordinating Group (2016). *Guide to Wildland Fire Origin and Cause Determination.* Boise, ID, USA.

Nordskog, E. (2013). *Fireraisers, Freaks and Fiends.* CreateSpace Independent Publishing Platform, SC, USA.

O'Connor, J.J. (1993). *Practical Fire and Arson Investigation.* CRC Press, Boca Raton, FL, USA.

Prestemon, J.P. & Butry, D.T. (2005). Time to burn: modelling wildland arson as an autoregressive crime function. *American Journal of Agricultural Economics,* 87(3), (pp. 756–770). American Agricultural Economics Association, Hanover, PA, USA.

Steensland, P. (n.d.). *Serial Wildland Arson Analysis.* [Unpublished manuscript]. Grants Pass, OR, USA.

Community engagement

6

Out of control wildfire in Sydney Australia (Photo taken by the author).

As is the case in solving and preventing crime, the engagement of the community is a vital part of the process. The information provided by local residents or motorists travelling through an area often provides valuable information to help identify an offender and to bring them to justice. Preventing and solving wildfire arson cases is no different.

However, experience suggests wildfire arson tends to be more common during daylight hours, when weather conditions are more conducive to successful fire spread, as opposed to the night-time period when lower temperatures, higher humidity and lower wind speeds may inhibit or prevent the successful ignition of vegetation fuels, whereas 'mainstream' criminal offences are more likely to be conducted under the concealment of darkness to avoid detection. A key part of wildfire investigation tactics is to promote the opportunity for the public to assist in the investigation by providing information about what they have observed in and around the scene of a wildfire prior to or after the ignition with this daylight timeframe in mind. This chapter highlights some options to promote this support not only from the community but also from first responder agency personnel.

DOI: 10.4324/9781003353843-7

Community engagement tactics

The details of measures to engage the community should be outlined in the MAA SOP document, which can also inform part of the Wildfire Investigation Incident Action Plan. This SOP should incorporate options for Community Education regarding wildfire arson awareness and prevention messaging, tailored to address the geographical area being targeted.

For instance, in urban-interface areas, local residents will have different access and observation opportunities to residents in a rural setting. Fire agencies are well versed in the engagement of their communities regarding wildfire mitigation and property protection measures. Budgets, staff and publications are focused to provide information on how to make homes and rural properties more wildfire resilient, often promoted through social media platforms and commercial television and radio. Many agencies are proactive in face-to-face engagement of their local community through public meetings leading into the fire season. This approach is often scaled up during peak times of increased fire danger. However, it is not common to see the message of wildfire arson prevention included in this message. More often, it only forms part of the messaging after a major fire event where it is suspected arson has taken place. Understandably, this message is often delivered at the same time the community is under the stress of evacuation preparation, road closure information and loss/damage reporting. Law enforcement seeks public information on 'suspicious persons and vehicles' seen in the vicinity of the fire and asks the public to report any information to authorities.

Pre-season wildfire safety messaging and advice should also contain information on the reality of wildfire arson. Acknowledging the risk in their community and providing residents and landholders with basic awareness tactics of how they can assist in tackling the issue should form part of the fire agency community engagement process. Basic information that is often sought during a wildfire emergency should be the basis of this messaging, for example, on days of heightened fire danger, asking community members to take note of and report vehicles or people, leading up to, during or immediately after the ignition of a wildfire. These observations may be more practical to note in the rural/urban interface, where residents are more familiar with local vehicles and the movements of neighbours. Nevertheless, a normal reaction is to dismiss this information to be trivial at the time prior to a wildfire occurring; therefore, it is critical to encourage the value any information has to preventing wildfire arson. Promoting the community to be part of the solution to preventing and detecting wildfire arson must be at the core of this message.

Importantly, an easy-to-access 'tip line' should accompany this messaging, to motivate the community to provide this information, even before a wildfire occurs.

Normally, a community's wildfire risk profile forms the basis of an agency's wildfire safety, prevention and mitigation messaging. The impact of this risk can be emphasised in this messaging when the increased risk posed by a deliberate ignition forms part of the community engagement campaign. This is seen as an ideal time to engage their assistance in being part of the arson prevention strategy by being part of the information gathering process before a wildfire occurs.

The resulting risks posed to the community and the linked response by emergency services can also be illustrated by any experience of the agency in their response and suppression of deliberately lit wildfires within the jurisdiction. Examples of past significant wildfires that resulted from the act of deliberately lighting a wildfire reinforce the need for community assistance in detecting wildfire arsonists, such as the 2002 Hayman Fire in Colorado in the United States that saw 138,000 acres (55,800 hectares) burn, 600 buildings lost and six indirect fatalities, deliberately lit by a former US Forest Service employee. And the Churchill Fire in Victoria in Australia in 2009, which saw 145 houses lost, 63,900 acres (25,861 hectares) burn, 11 fatalities deliberately lit by a 39-year-old local and one-time volunteer firefighter.

Urban-interface area strategy

Experience confirms that fire and law enforcement agencies are already engaged with their communities in their fire safety and policing roles. The extension of these roles should be to highlight their role in observing and noting people and vehicles in the area prior to and during a wildfire. Heightening their awareness of the need to record and be cognizant of issues that are 'out of the normal' can be valuable to the investigation. People entering and exiting reserves, vehicles driving in bushland areas and those who are bystanders after the fire is ignited are vital parts of information that may help solve a case. Reliable sources of information such as images from security cameras on residences, dash cameras in vehicles in the area and witness smartphone images or video can be of great value to the investigation. It is well known that many arsonists often return to fire scenes, so additional information may be obtained from bystanders during the fire suppression phase, and this may be uploaded to social media. Measures to encourage the public to be more mindful of recording, this information can be reinforced through existing community engagement channels; however, these initiatives can be enhanced if an area is subject to an ongoing arson series (Figure 6.1).

Rural area strategy

The approach by fire and law enforcement agencies in rural areas is somewhat similar; however, given the more isolated population, the ability to monitor all rural areas may be less practical. However, as is the case in mainstream

Figure 6.1 Arsonist who was later convicted, observed driving through an active investigation scene in Canada (Photograph taken by the author).

rural crime such as stock theft, there are still many occasions where information is offered by what is observed as being 'out of the ordinary'. Vehicles entering national parks and travelling on rural roads can often be noticed. Opportunities to engage with rural residents can also be channelled through traditional wildfire suppression agency avenues promoting fire safety or through similar lines via law enforcement awareness campaigns.

Many rural properties invest in CCTV equipment, and similar digital recording devices are fitted to rural vehicles, particularly those managed by farming corporations. Spreading the message about wildfire arson awareness is the key. Options to promote this message through local rural gatherings (e.g. stock saleyards) are likely to be known by agency investigators. Ultimately, the risk of economic loss through deliberately lit wildfires on grazing land or nearby reserves results in positive co-operation from rural communities.

General information sources

Social media are a valuable source of information and footage of wildfire events. The early-stage video of a wildfire can be extremely valuable to investigators to identify the General Origin Area and perhaps identify the arsonist as the camera operator. Investigators should check social media as part of their investigation process. Additionally, media crews may also possess extended time of video footage of the initial stages of the fire, particularly if the coverage includes news helicopter images, which may capture vehicles in and around the fire scene in its initial stages. Engagement of public news media outlets before the fire season to seek agreement to provide this footage to investigation teams as wildfires occur is also a positive tactic for information gathering. Agency access to satellite images is also rapidly evolving in many countries, providing high-definition images of areas of interest in the hours leading up to ignition. As access and detail offered by this technology become available, this data source will become more valuable to identify the precise location and events occurring at the wildfire ignition site.

As previously outlined, information can also be drawn from all witnesses via Crime Stoppers or 'Tip lines', which allow for anonymous information from the community. Often, this can be encouraged through the placement of signage in the area affected by the wildfire series (e.g. electronic roadside signs or permanent placards as depicted in Figure 6.2), along with press releases and media conferences to enhance investigation intelligence data.

Community engagement tactics using readily identifiable logos or images can form part of collaborative wildfire arson prevention campaigns, to be included in website messaging, social media streams from agencies and as messaging affixed to agency vehicles (such as the campaign run by the

Figure 6.2 Example of wildfire scene community information signage. NSW Rural Fire Service, Australia.

Figure 6.3A Examples of Wildfire Arson Prevention messaging. (A) Postcard by the Colorado Department of Fire Prevention and Control, (B) the United States Forest Service (reverse-sided vinyl license holder) and (C) vehicle sticker from the Australian Capital Territory Emergency Services Agency (developed by the author).

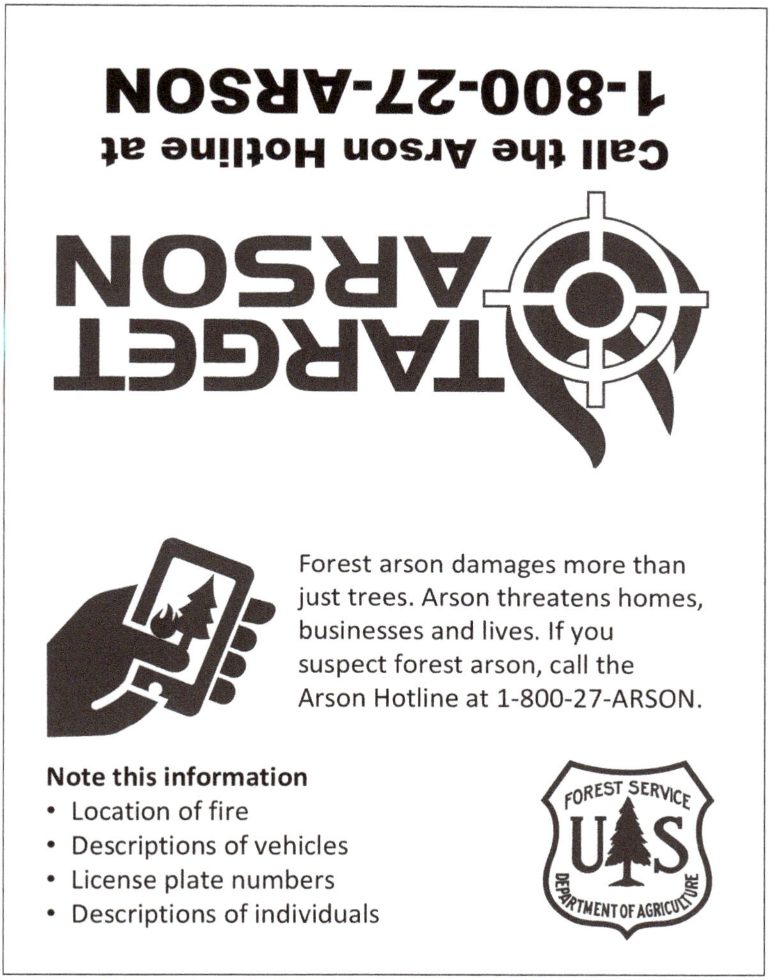

Figure 6.3B,C Examples of Wildfire Arson Prevention messaging. (A) Postcard by the Colorado Department of Fire Prevention and Control, (B) the United States Forest Service (reverse-sided vinyl license holder) and (C) vehicle sticker from the ACT Emergency Services Agency (developed by the author).

Colorado Department of Fire Prevention and Control and Australian Capital Territory Emergency Services Agency, as outlined in Figure 6.3 (as developed by the author in his fire service role). This proactive messaging provides an opportunity to remind the community to remain vigilant and acts as a reminder to responding agency officers, to seek out information from witnesses when on scene at an incident. It also sends a strong message as part of an awareness campaign to arsonists (and prospective arsonists), that deliberate fire lighting is a risk to life and property – and they will be caught and prosecuted.

Conclusion

The engagement of the community is vital to successfully addressing the problem of wildfire arson. When wildfires are featured in the media, members of all communities in wildfire-prone areas are very aware of their local risk from deliberate ignitions. Experience shows that many members of a local community are more than willing to become the eyes of the fire investigation team to help identify an arsonist. The promotion of wildfire arson prevention community engagement programs (e.g. if appropriate a community meeting, which may potentially identify the suspect in attendance) should be seen as a priority to be managed collaboratively, through the local Wildfire Arson Prevention Committee. Agency representatives are the best place to design a targeted program that best suits their area.

> Since the inception of the campaign, fire reporting has been shown to consistently increase across each of the three months most vulnerable to bushfires.
>
> *(Doley et al. 2016, p. 153) (In reference to the role of Crime Stoppers in wildfire arson information campaigns in Australia)*

Reference

Doley, R.M., Dickens, G.L. & Gannon, T.A. (2016). *The Psychology of Arson*. Routledge, Oxon, UK.

7 Firefighter arson

Volunteer Fire Station in The Netherlands (Photo taken by author).

The issue of firefighter arson affects all fire agencies and is often regarded as a 'sensitive topic' or a 'dirty little secret'. Similar to police corruption, it strikes at the heart of the reputation of fire agencies whose ultimate goal is to keep their communities safe. But when it surfaces the public trust in the fire agency is severely damaged and the community perception of the organisation's ethics, honesty and reliability rapidly erodes. There are many different attitudes from the leadership of fire agencies around the world as to how the problem is managed. Some take an attitude of declaring it does not exist and, therefore, there is no action needed to be taken; some only act after offenders are coincidentally identified within their ranks, choosing to transfer or demand their resignation without taking further action. Others take a more proactive approach in varying degrees to have fire incidents investigated and links to firefighters explored as part of the investigation process.

Nevertheless, it is recognised that it is an issue that many fire agencies would rather not exist. Therefore, the intent must be to establish adequate prevention and detection measures based on best practice strategies and tactics, to protect the good reputation of the majority of firefighters who also view firefighter arson as an act of betrayal against their reputation.

DOI: 10.4324/9781003353843-8

How big is the issue of wildfire firefighter arson?

Research in the area of firefighter arson is very limited. The research into wildfire firefighter arson is even more limited. Reports are essentially based on those who have been caught and convicted, with inadequate research and follow-up evident. Once the firefighter is convicted and terminated from the agency the problem is deemed to be 'gone'. However, this reaction is understandable as most agencies are keen to remove the problem to protect the good work the majority of their personnel do in protecting their communities and the natural environment. But as a result, there is not a good appreciation of the scope of the problem and more research is needed to fully understand it. The limited research that has been undertaken has found similar trends of the small number involved in those to date is acknowledged by retired United States FBI Analyst for the National Center for the Analysis of Violent Crime, Tim Huff,

> The number of known cases is relatively small, considering the approximately one million paid and volunteer fire fighters in this country. Thankfully, the overwhelming majority of fire fighters dedicate their lives to serving their communities and richly deserve the hero status they often achieve.
>
> *(Huff 1994, p. 1)*

Another Australian-based study looking at the problem in 2003 also confirmed the limited size of the issue compared with the total number of firefighter numbers,

> Perhaps the most important point to make about the incidence or frequency of arson committed by firefighters is that it is extremely rare when viewed against the number of firefighters who never commit arson. Of course, the 75 firefighters identified by the USFA as maliciously lighting fires is 75 too many. Nonetheless, this is but a tiny fraction of the over one million volunteer and paid firefighters operating in the United States (USFA 2003: 5).
>
> *(Willis 2004, p. 99)*

It is also recognised that firefighter arsonists also report the cause of their fires as within agency incident reports as 'unknown' to cover their activities (Figure 7.1). The author had experience while managing wildfire investigations on behalf of the largest rural firefighting agency in Australia to address a series of deliberately lit wildfires across two consecutive fire seasons. This arrangement saw him working closely alongside law enforcement determining the cause of wildfires after severe seasons in the early 2000s,

> In Australia, Strikeforce Tronto, set up by NSW Police to investigate the causes of bushfires in that State, investigated some 1,600 suspicious fires in its first

Figure 7.1 Every successful wildfire ignition initiated by a firefighter can result in significant risk to fellow responding firefighters and the community (Photograph taken by the author).

> three years of operation (Warne-Smith 2004:3). Through those investigations 50 people were charged, 11 of them volunteer members of the NSW Rural Fire Service.
>
> *(Willis 2004, p. 99)*

This equates to 22% of all individuals charged being firefighters. This organisation, which has a primary role of managing wildfires, had in the vicinity of 70,000 volunteer members; therefore, the number of convicted members represented a very small fraction of the majority who were serving their community in dealing with one of the most challenging fire seasons at that time. Notably, this percentage is in line with findings in the United States where Steensland cites a 1994 FBI study (Fire Setting Fire Fighters: Arsonists in the Fire Department-Identification and Prevention), which looked at the background of arsonists, "A study of 25 firefighter arson cases involving 75 offenders, conducted by the FBI… The fact that firefighters made up 32% of this study sample, however, should be viewed as potentially significant by wildland fire investigators" (Steensland n.d., p. 45). Given these findings, a focus of an investigation should also involve the firefighters who have responded to wildfires in the area under investigation.

Most wildfire agencies pride themselves on keeping their community safe (given it is common for members to also reside in these communities). However, it is possible that limited detection rates may also hide the extent of the problem in some jurisdictions. How many firefighters have successfully lit wildfires without ever being detected in their careers? How many of these incidents resulted in death and destruction? This aspect can only be imagined. The experience of the author during the 1990s supervising volunteer fire departments (ranging from 300 to 1,200 members across a range of jurisdictions and levels of wildfire risk), exposed clusters of unusually higher rates of deliberately lit fires in towns and urban interface areas. The possibility of firefighter arson was high on the radar as a result. The task of identifying these individuals in a fire agency (which at the time, did not have any consistent reporting or investigation mechanisms) proved challenging. Logically, law enforcement was engaged to identify those responsible. However, investigations remained largely unresolved during a period of limited wildfire investigation knowledge and expertise. This was against a landscape of isolated tight-knit communities, which was reflected in small numbers of firefighter members at each station. It was not until intelligence sharing between the agencies, the adoption of a formal investigation of fire scenes and a joint approach with law enforcement was initiated, saw this situation turned around. The author was later promoted to a position to establish and manage the investigation of fires across the whole of this State agency, which resulted in a more consistent State-wide approach to more actively address the possibility of firefighter arson, supported by clear and consistent procedures as recommended in this guide.

One of the most positive aspects of the leadership of rural fire stations is their ability to know what is happening in their local area. For example, their knowledge of the number of responses over time to local wildfire events over time places them in a strong position to identify 'unexplained' increases in ignitions. Against a backdrop of pride to protect their community and prevent wildfire risk to their areas, they are often a reliable source of intelligence in the absence of more formal incident analysis monitoring and investigation of fire scenes. Based on experience, the identification of the wildfire cause and those responsible is now more often viewed seriously by these crew leaders and any possible involvement of new recruits in fire lighting.

Regardless of the perceived extent of the activity in an area, deliberate lighting of fires by firefighters is a problem. The 'fire agency membership profiles' that may be more at risk are unclear. But taking action is the key to ensuring it is not a risk to the community our firefighters serve must be a part of the solution. "There is a problem, we cannot ignore the problem, we must talk to our members about firefighter arson. We must investigate, charge, and convict those that are committing this crime (NVFC, 1994)" (NVFC 2011, p. 9).

Why do firefighters light wildfires?

The element that firefighters are trained in understanding the issues influencing wildfire behaviour, places the firefighter arson in an ideal position to set the size of their fires and limited risk outcomes to meet the desired goal. For instance, a firefighter's basic training course commonly includes theory on wildfire behaviour, providing an understanding between fuel, weather and topography. It follows that this knowledge is valuable for firefighter arsonists to limit their wildfire ignitions to smaller areas, so tactics such as igniting their fires on Low Fire Danger Rating days, at the top of a slope, with low fuel loads will result in their fires having a slow rate of spread, low fire intensity and unlikely to cause any risk to the property. Ultimately, these 'nuisance' wildfires are easily controlled through their response with their fellow fire crew members. The firefighters may be seeking the excitement of responding to a wildfire, applying their learnt skills, and the member is emotionally 'rewarded' in extinguishing a minor fire, which is unlikely to be investigated. The more fires the individuals ignite, the greater their understanding and confidence they have in the likely results, honing their skills from each fire event. Similarly, armed with their fire behaviour knowledge, a firefighter arsonist may also target days of heightened fire danger, ignition locations at the base of hilly terrain, with high fuel loads, to maximise the resulting rate of spread and intensity of the fire and to limit the success of suppression employed by responding crews (Figure 7.2).

Additionally, experience has shown that there have been a number of cases in Australia where the firefighter arsonist has misjudged the conditions or timing of the delayed ignition device, which resulted in an uncontrollable fire impacting nearby assets and placing lives at risk. Their planned 'minor fire' exceeds their understanding of the parameters on the day resulting in an 'unintended' major wildfire event.

Figure 7.2 Wildfire suppression agency vehicle in South Korea (Photograph taken by the author).

The commonly recognised causes of wildfire arson already detailed are described by the FBI as excitement, vandalism, revenge, profit, extremism and crime concealment. However, when they considered the motives of firefighter arsonists, it was found "...the primary motives for firefighter arson seem to be the need to be *seen as a hero*, to practice extinguishing fires, or to earn extra money" (FEMA 2003, p. 8).

Financial gain can be linked to firefighters who are monetarily rewarded for the more fires they attend. By lighting minor wildfires that are rapidly extinguished, a regular income stream is provided to supplement that provided through full-time jobs in their local communities. Lightning wildfires during periods of low fire activity guarantee this income. There may also be a perception by the firefighter that setting fire to an acre of grassland is less risky than lighting a dumpster located near structures in the town area.

Hero status within the fire agency is often a motive that sees newly recruited firefighters lighting wildfires (Figure 7.3). Engineering an opportunity to

Figure 7.3 Motive of being a 'hero' in the eyes of their community or by their peers, is often found as a trigger in firefighter arsonists. Firefighter suppressing a wildfire in the Netherlands (Photograph taken by the author).

prove themselves in front of their peers is seen as a way of becoming accepted within the local fire station hierarchy. In many smaller jurisdictions where the number of wildfire incidents is typically low, this prospect may not arise for months or even years, for the newly trained recruit to prove his or her ability to extinguish a fire. So logically by lighting a wildfire, the event presents them with a chance to prove themselves. This was experienced in a fire department in the State of Pennsylvania in the United States,

> They're generally younger, in their teens or early 20s. They entered the fire service expecting a lot of excitement and that's typically not the case. They say, 'We haven't fought a fire in six months. Let's go start one'... They think they have to prove themselves to somebody.
>
> *(Finley 2008 as cited by Hinds-Aldrich in IFSJLM 2011, p. 36)*

A key aspect of this category is being perceived as a hero by their local community. "Firefighters are known to set fires so they can engage in the suppression effort. Firefighter arsonists who seek recognition, or wish to be viewed as heroes, may set and "discover" the fires" (FEMA 2003, p. 9). A case in Australia where this occurred saw the young recruit promote his volunteer firefighting role in his private life by wearing his fire uniform to parties and having newspaper cuttings of firefighters at major fire events adorn his bedroom wall. Often, it is not the act of suppressing a fire but the urgent response on the fire truck through the town that satisfies this motive (Figure 7.4).

A readily accessible opportunity to promote their hero status is also available through social media. Instead of bragging at the bar about how they stopped the wildfire and saved the community, a couple of posts of images

Figure 7.4 Firefighters extinguishing a wildfire in the Netherlands (Photograph taken by the author).

and stories of the courageous effort can be transmitted to the world to satisfy this motive and to shine the spotlight on their role in saving the town.

Revenge may also be encountered in firefighters lighting fires. Taking out a grievance against an individual or their agency may be a trigger as was found in the United States, "Disgruntled employees of the fire service may set fires in retaliation for a perceived grievance" (FEMA 2003, p. 9). A firefighter overlooked for promotion, reduction in funding to replace ageing equipment or closure of fire stations may be a trigger for a motive involving revenge firefighter arson against their agency.

Extremist/terrorist-related motives are emerging across a number of countries in wildfire events. However, the infiltration of an individual into a wildfire management agency to learn the craft in how to successfully light a wildfire event to have maximum damage and destruction is yet to emerge in the author's experience. Nevertheless, it should not be discounted.

Crime concealment is a motive commonly encountered in structural fire arson; however, experience in wildfire cause suggests this tends to be mainly limited to stolen and dumped motor vehicles that are deliberately set fire with the vehicle fire subsequently spreading to the surrounding vegetation. The incidence of concealing evidence associated with cases of homicide by burning the body can also be encountered. There are very limited cases of firefighters associated with this motive, but needs to be considered in relation to associated evidence.

Mixed motives should also be considered as concluded in the FEMA Study. An example was experienced by the author in an investigation of a long-term wildfire agency Divisional Commander. A 22-year veteran officer aged in his late 30s was in the role of mentoring a younger female firefighter, assigned to him to assist in his Divisional Commander role. She had previously expressed her frustration to him of not having experienced a 'code-3' response to a wildfire. On the day of the fire, he had initially 'staged' a telephone call while in the Dispatch Centre, enabling him to be involved in a planned 'code-3' response to the location of a 'reported' wildfire (he initially stated was from a hiker). The location in the first response was attended by several fire units along with the commander and proved (initially), to be a 'false alarm.' Around 10 minutes after leaving the scene, a legitimate report of a wildfire at the same location was received, which saw the fire units return to the scene to find a rapidly spreading wildfire threatening property and lives, on a day of heightened fire danger. In this case, it was never proven if he had personally lit the wildfire or had someone light it on his behalf. However, during the investigation, the officer finally confessed to having been the initial caller to the Dispatch Center he 'answered,' after the audio record exposed him speaking on a vacant telephone line to a non-existent caller as he 'recorded details' of the fire 'incident'. After a comprehensive investigation he was to be charged with arson, however prosecutors declined the charge due to a lack of evidence. He was subsequently convicted of 'hindering an investigation' and dismissed from the fire agency. It also was found during the investigation that he had recently been denied a promotion to a more senior role and resented his supervisor for this decision (revenge?); his peers also commented to investigators of his open commentary to members on his fascination with fire and his frustration when no wildfire incidents occurred on days of heightened fire danger (excitement?). Notably, the area had been subject to a number of minor wildfires resulting from serial arson events over a number of years, which ceased after this investigation closed.

Prevention policy and tactics

Experience has shown that most fire agencies have very limited policies and procedures for investigating wildfire arsonists within their ranks. Unrealistic perceptions that are often heard such as, 'it is not a problem in our organisation', or 'when we find out we have a problem the case is referred to law enforcement', are common. When a firefighter arsonist is identified in the circumstances, agency leadership often scramble damage control of the exposure of the organisation to the crime, placing the agency under pressure to deflect criticism of one of their own is identified as lighting fires they attend. Political and media reaction exacerbates this problem, particularly when the agency is lacking a well-defined policy and procedures to prevent the problem in the first place.

Screening of recruits

The first logical stage is to scene potential firefighters for previous arson convictions. While this is a start, it will not identify those who may be listed on intelligence databases suspected of wildfire arson. It is also recognised that these criminal checks have limitations, "However, we cannot put too much faith in background checks alone - as a number of recent cases have shown. In fact, Tim Huff, a former analyst with the FBI Academy in the United States, also noted that 'most of the group offenders appeared not to have the inclination to set any fires before joining the department. The idea occurred to them later.'" (Huff 1994 as cited by Hinds-Aldrich in IFSJLM 2011, pp. 40–41). This is understandable, as experience shows arsonist firefighters are not likely to set fires until they are presented with an opportunity and motive once they are part of the wildfire agency. To supplement recruitment procedures, some agencies have adopted internal psychological screening of recruits to identify those who may be at risk of lighting fires. In New Zealand, a firefighter selection and screening interview process was introduced to identify an individual's propensity to light fires along with identifying a specific range of behavioural characteristics to ensure the applicant successfully transitions into their role in the fire service.

As Dr. Rebekah Doley, a Criminal Behaviour Analyst and Psychologist specialising in the analysis of arsonists, found "…the questionnaire doesn't offer an absolute predictable of arson propensity, but instead compares a subject's response with characteristics of the volunteer arsonist profile" (Doley 2003, p. 68). The adoption of an enhanced and targeted screening process to identify those who may be deemed unsuitable should be considered, particularly in volunteer firefighting agencies. In some agencies, this may seem to be impractical where recruitment is locally managed; however, in South Carolina in the United States, a recruitment psychological assessment tool is used by fire service staff focusing on eight key areas through 40 questions over a 30-minute assessment, using a scaled response criteria to identify behavioural tendencies common in firefighter arsonists. Agencies need to recognise a small investment in the prevention of firefighter wildfire arson can assist in keeping their community and staff safe. Experience shows the consequences of not screening recruits can have devastating consequences for the community and the agency.

Another key aspect is to cross reference the applicant's previous fire service history. This can be particularly challenging where fire agencies are independently governed across different jurisdictional models. If a firefighter has been dismissed from one agency due to a conviction of arson or even suspicion of arson and applies to join a different department without disclosing their previous experience, they will likely 'slip through the net'. This has been experienced by the author and has been seen in investigations in the United States. A previously convicted wildfire firefighter was able to join a small volunteer department to fulfil his desire to be a hero in a fire station serving his community. After being accepted into the agency and responding to fires, it was only when investigators visited the fire station by chance that they recognised the convicted arsonist in uniform, "His application, like many across the nation for volunteer firefighters, asked no questions about his criminal background. He simply told them he had no firefighting experience and wished to help" (Nordskog 2013, p. 268). Understandably, this small community, like many around the world, was keen to accept any new members to ensure they could continue to maintain their response capability; however, avenues to conduct background checks must be facilitated on a national basis. Experience in Australia also saw a convicted arsonist who was dismissed from a fire agency in one State, move several States to try to join another fire agency. It was only through personal contacts between the agencies at the time that the name of the individual rang alarm bells and his application was immediately rejected.

Zero tolerance policy

Experience has shown a robust policy of 'zero tolerance' to firefighter arson needs to be implemented and importantly, enforced. Similar to law enforcement corruption prevention policy, it must be promoted to all firefighters at recruitment, training and in agency doctrine. The policy must

- be easily implemented and understood;
- enable members at all ranks to easily access a confidential reporting process;
- clearly articulate disciplinary ramifications to members who fail to report their suspicions of fellow members who are lighting wildfires and
- emphasise that the agency will not support members who are suspected of lighting wildfires and they will be subject to criminal proceedings.

The support of the membership, executive and chief of the agency is essential to the success of this policy. A high-profile message campaign needs to be evident as part of this policy. For example, intranet messaging linking to policy and reporting portals; posters in fire stations (similar to the one in Figure 7.5 and integration of this messaging in agency publications on an ongoing basis).

The membership status of the firefighter charged with arson must be included in this policy, which should see his suspended pending legal processes. All members must understand that their career as a firefighter will be terminated if convicted of wildfire arson (Figure 7.5).

Training

All firefighters undertake wildfire suppression, wildfire behaviour and firefighting equipment use and the like, as part of their recruitment training. A highlight of this training should also include a reference to the reality of firefighter arson, along with reinforcement of the agency's zero tolerance policy. It has been found that this must form part of the recruit firefighter's initial training package, to ensure it is clearly understood that the agency will investigate any suggestion of firefighter arson and that members will face serious criminal charges, along with dismissal from the agency. This material should also detail confidential reporting channels available for all members, should they have suspicions of it occurring. The author incorporated this message into wildfire scene preservation training material which is now delivered to at least two agencies in Australia. A version of this is now included in the NWCG "FI-110, Wildland Fire Observations and Origin Scene Protection for

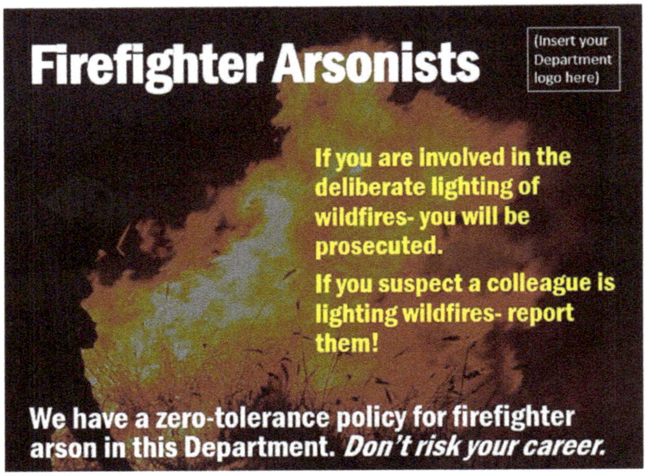

Figure 7.5 Example of a Firefighter Arson prevention poster designed by the author.

First Responders" 2021 edition, as highlighted in Figure 7.6. Leadership training courses should also embed details of how to identify firefighter arsonists within the agency ranks with a focus on pattern analysis, firefighter response trends, unusual levels of incident knowledge by a firefighter during response phases and traits such as an unusual level of interest in wildfire or enthusiasm for response opportunities. Again, an emphasis on the agency's zero tolerance policy needs to form part of this awareness process.

Media

Understandably, experience shows that media interest is generally high after a firefighter has been charged with lighting wildfires. The perception of a "black eye" to the agency cannot be dodged. But the charging of a firefighter with wildfire arson should be seen as an opportunity to promote the agency's zero tolerance policy regarding firefighter arson. It should be promoted to the media as a positive result of internal investigation processes working to identify firefighter arsonists, along with collaboration arrangements with law enforcement to detect firefighter arsonists. It also sends a firm message to all firefighters that the agency is serious about dealing with this issue. Agencies should also have responses prepared for these events along with an all-staff advice notification to underscore the zero tolerance message. This approach should be part of the agency policy doctrine detailing strategies and tactics to prevent and detect firefighter arsonists.

Studies have shown that a proactive approach in this respect pays dividends to the agency if/when a firefighter arsonist is detected and charged.

Figure 7.6 The issue of firefighter arson as highlighted in the FI-110 Training Course, developed by the National Wildfire Co-ordinating Group (National Wildfire Co-ordinating Group, 2021).

Investigating wildfire firefighter arsonists

Typically, experience suggests in identifying where to start to investigate wildfire events, the assumption is not one of considering if a local firefighter as being behind the cause of wildfires plaguing the area. 'Why would a firefighter light a wildfire? Their role is to protect the community and national park?' Often initially overlooked by investigators, the signs and evidence of firefighter arson are often already present and easily identified.

The key component to investigating firefighters suspected of being arsonists is confidentiality. There are many cases where the in-house fire agency network of 'trust' has been broken mid-investigation, and lack of evidence prohibits any legal action against the officer, and the case is closed.

First signs of a firefighter arsonist

One common trait that may indicate the first signs of a wildfire arsonist in the ranks, is the firefighter who continually calls in wildfires they 'discover'. A simple exercise of asking career firefighters of how many fires they have come across and reported in their career, rarely sees extensive numbers… one or two tends to be the norm. After a firefighter reports two or more fires in a short period of time, the focus of an investigation on the individual needs to be seriously considered, particularly if they subsequently go out of their way to form part of the response crew. A broader review of the telephone numbers used to call in other incidents from anonymous callers should also be considered, based on a geospatial review of the locations of wildfires in relation to those reported by the firefighter. Additional hoax calls should also make up this analysis and a firefighter having a second mobile telephone should also be considered in these circumstances. Another sign of anonymous emergency callers that may be linked to a firefighter is the use of wildfire terminology used. For example, "I am reporting a wildfire in the Watson Reserve. It looks like it may cause *spot fires* across the river, so the fire department may need to respond to a *medium helicopter and at least 3 tankers*". Emergency Dispatch Center supervisors should be made aware of these to highlight these incidents to investigators.

A geospatial review must also form the starting point of the investigation within the fire district response area boundary and outside of it, to identify likely opportunities for a station to respond to the incident within their station's area of responsibility. A broad analysis of all incidents across an agency jurisdiction will soon expose clusters against all other station response areas.

A temporal analysis reviewing the times of the day, days of the week and days of the month when wildfires occurred, against the crew members' response and availability will also be valuable to validate members' available and non-available days. A pattern here of aligned availability with incident trends may also provide additional evidence of an arsonist in the ranks.

Response times of members should also be analysed against the reported timing of wildfire events. In a volunteer unit, a member is the first to attend the station continually, against what would normally be expected under member response times, and may also be evidence of prior knowledge of the ignition. There have been cases when the immediate response of firefighters to a station became obvious that they would move the fire tanker out of the engine bay prior to the station being called out for the incident.

Additionally, a member having an intimate knowledge of the location of a reported wildfire guiding the crew leader to the scene may also be a red flag of an issue. The author had experience with an investigation of a firefighter who after completing his training, was continually pestering his crew leader to be included in the next call-out. The member lived some distance away from the fire station and, therefore, was unlikely to be able to attend in time to be on the first tanker response. Eventually, he did get a call and happened to attend the station in time for the response. Nearing the scene, he provided the crew with a commentary of the 'likely' access to the wildfire off a roadway in a national park. He confirmed the fire trail access; however, at the time, the then low-intensity fire was downwind of his vehicle and obscured by the height of vegetation. Impossible to view from the roadway, the crew leader immediately became suspicious and reported his concerns to his supervisor. During questioning of the firefighter at the scene, he stated that he had observed smoke and fire while on the roadway, hence his directions to the crew leader. Pointing out the location from where he first saw the fire, his version of events fell apart when it was confirmed his supposed clear view up the fire trail would not have been possible before the fire had spread, as this modified field of view was only possible after the vegetation had subsequently burnt, well after his crew had attempted initial attack. He was subsequently charged with lighting the wildfire and dismissed from the agency.

Therefore, the examination of all wildfire scenes is critical in the investigation process when a pattern of ignitions emerges to validate or refute firefighter versions of events. Experience shows firefighter arsonists tend to drive to their selected remote locations where they light their fires, using delay devices to allow them sufficient time to return to the vicinity of their fire station to be on the first responding vehicle. The examinations are essential to detect evidence and commonality, such as tire impressions, footprints or remnants of delay devices to recover fingerprints or DNA. Linking commonly constructed recovered devices from scenes can then form the basis of a later search of a firefighter's vehicle and residence for similar devices or materials (Figure 7.7).

Understandably, the use of a delay device is critical to ensure that the firefighter has adequate time to be in the vicinity of their station when the fire ignites and the fire is reported. The rank of firefighter arsonists also needs to be considered. The majority of those convicted appear to be newer recruits. However, career officers may also justify their fire lighting to ensure their area's fire event statistics are high to justify the need for additional resources or budgets and should also be considered as part of an analysis process.

A further consideration is the deliberate destruction of the Specific Origin Area in suppression operations by firefighters. Obviously, firefighters who are trained in scene preservation will be keen to destroy any evidence of their fire lighting through the use of excessive volumes and pressure of waterlines, unnecessary deployment of heavy plant and driving of fire vehicles over the area's first discovered burning.

Arson in company with other members should also not be discounted. The correlation of members with close relationships outside the station and attending the fire station around the same time on an ongoing basis may suggest collusion in fire lighting. The reporting of wildfire outbreaks by a select group of members of the station is likely an indication of fire lighting amongst members. Often, this can be part of a peer pressure scenario to ensure that the station is active or can be an initiation exercise for new recruits, 'we all had to do it'.

Intelligence gathering by station supervisors/crew leaders is often a vital step as part of the tactics to be employed. Trustworthy and longstanding members can be useful in gathering information on the movements, behaviour and any likely information that may implicate a

Figure 7.7 Wildfire scene examinations are a vital part of identifying firefighter arsonists. Alberta, Canada (Photograph taken by the author).

firefighter involved in deliberate fire lighting. The author had experience in relying on an experienced and well-regarded station supervisor, who kept a diary documenting the movements and timings of a later convicted firefighter arsonist who lit wildfires in the response area of his station. This information was critical in refuting the member's version of events and the stated timing of his attendance at the fire station prior to the report of a wildfire. Importantly, the sensitivities and trustworthiness of these members need to be very carefully assessed, along with the need for confidentiality.

Tactics for investigations

Once a firefighter suspect comes to the notice of the agency, investigations should follow a previously agreed joint investigation plan applicable to the jurisdiction. The involvement of fire agency investigators is critical in this model, to ensure their skills are embedded in the investigation process, along with providing timely wildfire event information and evidence. Law enforcement specialist roles will likely also extend to specialist criminal investigation tactics (e.g. surveillance of the firefighter suspect). The use of GPS tracking devices is a reliable tactic to employ in identifying the movements of a suspected firefighter arsonist, particularly when they are placed at the scene of an ignition prior to it being reported to their agency.

Similar tactics as previously mentioned along with other technologies outlined in Chapter 5, such as the use of covert cameras on roadways and trails where clusters have been identified to align the firefighter with fire activity, will form part of the investigation. Other technology such as vehicle licence plate recognition cameras can be valuable in identifying vehicles owned by the firefighter in and around the scene of wildfires prior to the events being reported. It is important to recognise some investigation tactics may be challenging to implement in small rural communities, in particular, to maintain confidentiality and security in a village setting where the firefighter is based. A flexible approach is needed to ensure the tactics suit the investigation environment. As such, the investigation team may need to be located in an adjoining town, operating for example in rented premises under a pseudo-audit operation 'disguise'. The use of unmarked rental vehicles (ages, makes and models that are specifically selected to ensure they blend in with the local community), may also form part of the investigation, with key investigators from another part of the jurisdiction or from an outside agency to maintain inconspicuous operations during the investigation phase.

Another key to confirming the involvement of the firefighter is the linkage of evidence from the wildfire scene/s to evidence located in the officer's vehicle or at their residence. Legally conducted searches are vital to locating this evidence, to locate and link materials used in constructing delay devices secreted in vehicles and at the homes of firefighters, along with proof of purchase at retail outlets. Cases the author has been involved in saw evidence on CCTV recovered from businesses where the officer purchased matches, mosquito coils and the like, which were also located at their home residence, linking those recovered at fire scenes.

One of the most challenging aspects of the investigation of firefighter arsonists is to know when to arrest the member. Do you have enough evidence to charge them based on applicable legislation? Is the officer igniting fires in concert with fellow firefighters? Is there sufficient evidence to arrest them sooner rather than later, to prevent them from lighting another fire which may expose the community and fellow firefighters to further risk? Are the suspicions of the agency investigators, just a coincidence as being a keen member of the fire service? These challenges need to be considered in all wildfire Investigations and equally apply to investigating firefighter arsonists and will influence the tactics adopted.

Interviewing the firefighter arsonist

The interview process must also be planned and undertaken by law enforcement and experienced fire agency investigators. Fire agency investigators are valuable as they have an intimate knowledge of the workings of the fire agency response processes and procedures, along with an understanding of the evolution of each incident along with wildfire behaviour. If not located in the interview room, they should be in an adjoining room monitoring the interview and the responses of the firefighter. Their role is essential in this process, as a law enforcement investigator who is not familiar with fire agency processes can miss vital facts which may implicate the firefighter's prior knowledge of the wildfire, based on their role in the fire agency. Importantly, the interview team must have knowledge of the fire scene examination findings, key linkage of evidence of the firefighter to each scene, the precise location of the Ignition Area, weather conditions at the time of the ignition, fire behaviour and key aspects of the initial stages of the wildfire, to challenge or confirm the responses from the firefighter.

Taking the firefighter to each fire scene is also a vital part of the interview process, recording their recollection of events and having them describe what they did and saw. Asked what they were doing in the area, how they became aware of the wildfire, showing their location when they first detected it, how they were assigned to their fire station response, their role on the suppression crew and their suppression tactics at the scene. Where they parked their vehicle, the location they admit lighting the fire (or if they deny their involvement, their description of the fire scene when they arrived or first discovered the fire), can assist in validating the facts of the case. If they are the reporting party, a description of the area that was burning, the fire intensity and the location of the Advancing, Backing and Lateral Vectors of the fire on their arrival, are all valuable information to compare the findings of the fire scene examination findings. These on-site interviews can often provide clues to their involvement in lighting the wildfire and can validate the findings of the scene investigation, providing evidence of their honesty to the interviewing investigators.

The approach of investigators will depend on the evidence involved in each case. However, success in past cases has mainly occurred after the firefighter is put at ease, details of the case are intimately known by the investigating officers and the firefighter is provided with critical details of evidence that results in a full confession. They may even admit to lighting additional wildfires that investigators have not considered, in what can be a very confronting time in the firefighter's involvement in their career within the agency.

Conclusion

The next wildfire a firefighter lights has the potential to cost the life of a fellow firefighter or a member of their community and result in damage or destruction of property. The issue of firefighter arson is well recognised around the world as a problem for fire agencies to address. Taking a proactive approach as part of the jurisdiction's Wildfire Arson Prevention Plan, the issue can be proactively tackled to identify and convict those few who chose to bring their colleagues and the name of their agency into disrepute.

> Firefighter arson is a cancer that can be cured. Taking a stand against this problem is the only practical way to reveal illegal conduct or major abuses of public authority and represents the highest form of loyalty to the fire service and its mission. Remember that in this venue, practicing the "art of avoidance" only gives victory to criminal action and improper conduct.
>
> *(Aurnhammer as cited by Lindroth 2003, p. 10)*

References

Doley, R.M. (2003). *Smoke Screen.* 'Fire Chief' Magazine. Chicago, IL, USA.

Federal Emergency Management Agency (FEMA) (2003). *Firefighter Arson Special Report. Technical Report Series 141.* United States Fire Administration, Emmitsburg, MA, USA.

Hinds-Aldrich, M. (2011). Firesetting firefighters: reconsidering a persistent problem. *International Fire Service Journal of Leadership and Management*, (Vol. 5), (pp. 33–46). Oklahoma State University, Stillwater, OK, USA.

Huff, T. (1994). *Fire-Setting Fire Fighters: Arsonists in the Fire Department – 'On-Scene'.* International Association of Fire Chiefs, Chantilly, VA, USA.

Lindroth, R. (2003). *Firefighter Arson, Recovery after Betrayal.* Livermore Fire Protection District, Livermore, CO, USA.

National Volunteer Fire Council (2011). *Report on the Firefighter Arson Problem: Context, Considerations, and Best Practices.* Greenbelt, MD, USA.

National Wildfire Co-ordinating Group (2021). *FI-110 Wildland Fire Observations and Origin Scene Protection for First Responders Course*. Boise, ID, USA.

Nordskog, E. (2013). *Fireraisers, Freaks and Fiends*. CreateSpace Independent Publishing Platform, SC, USA.

Steensland, P. (n.d.). *Serial Wildland Arson Analysis*. [Unpublished manuscript]. Grants Pass, OR, USA.

Willis, M. (2004). *Bushfire Arson: A Review of the Literature*. Australian Institute of Criminology, Canberra, ACT, Australia.

Training

8

Author presenting at an FI-210 Wildland Fire Origin and Cause Determination Course in Guam. Mariana Islands (Photo taken by Jeff Henricks, Canada).

To successfully identify and prosecute serial wildfire arsonists, it is highly recommended that investigators working under the Wildfire Arson Prevention Committee MOU enhance their skills in this specialist area of investigation. Undergoing accredited, specialised training provides them with industry-best practice skills to apply to their jurisdictional circumstances. The NWCG has developed three levels of training that are aligned to address the hierarchy of officers (from the frontline firefighter, fire scene examiners to locate the origin and cause of a wildfire to the investigation team involved in a complex investigation of a significant wildfire event or of serial arson).

The details of the agreed minimum training and qualification requirements should be outlined in the MAA SOP document, as approved by the Wildfire Arson Prevention Committee. Ideally, these standards should be in line with internationally recognised best practice training programmes, such as those offered by the NWCG.

Traditionally, law enforcement training has not provided focused wildfire arson investigation specialist skill enhancement. Mainstream structure fire scene examination and investigation techniques are more commonly provided. Similarly, fire agencies focus much of their frontline training on fire suppression,

DOI: 10.4324/9781003353843-9

Figure 8.1 A competent wildfire scene examination relies on the investigator having a thorough appreciation of wildfire behaviour to successfully locate the origin (Photograph taken by the author in Alberta, Canada).

and prevention techniques and strategies versus specific wildfire cause determination and investigation skills. This emphasis needs to shift in jurisdictions exposed to the risk of wildfire. Experience has shown that the upskilling of fire and law enforcement officers in wildfire investigation provides significant benefits in the prevention and prosecution of wildfire arson events (Figure 8.1).

What training is applicable?

The North American–based NWCG has developed wildfire investigation-specific courses, written by a collective team from key wildfire-prone countries such as the United States of America, Canada, Australia and New Zealand. The courses are, therefore, designed to apply across international jurisdictions in varying fuel types and in countries with differing levels of wildfire risk. It is essential that these levels of skill enhancement are provided to those who have the responsibility to address the wildfire arson problem. Experience has shown that investigators from jurisdictions who do not possess these specialist skills do not successfully reduce the rate of unplanned wildfire ignitions and rarely identify or convict those who are responsible.

First response crews

As previously mentioned, the responsibilities of firefighters in fire investigations go beyond just extinguishing the fire. They are considered reliable

Figure 8.2 First-attending fire crews, such as this one in New South Wales, Australia, must have an understanding of the importance to preserve evidence of the cause of the wildfire they suppress, New South Wales, Australia (photograph taken by the author).

witnesses to the early stages of the fire and have a major role in managing the preservation of evidence at a wildfire scene. They also have an important role in accurately identifying and reporting on the cause of the wildfires they routinely attend. They are also vital in the identification and preservation of the wildfire scene.

The recommended training course for these officers is the 'FI-110 Wildland Fire Observations and Origin Scene Protection for First Responders'. It is designed to provide fire crews with the skills to undertake origin scene protection measures to ensure that evidence is not damaged or destroyed relating to identifying the cause. It also provides basic wildfire cause identification skills. It is facilitated over six hours via classroom or online delivery (Figure 8.2).

Fire scene investigators

Accredited wildfire scene investigators have the responsibility to examine fire scenes to identify the origin and cause of a wildfire. They must have a good appreciation of wildfire behaviour and causes of wildfires. They also play a key role in identifying who is responsible for the ignition. The recommended training for these officers is the 'FI-210 Wildland Fire Origin and Cause Determination Course'. This course provides the skills for experienced fire service, land management and law enforcement crime scene officers to examine a wildfire scene and identify the origin and cause of the wildfire using fire pattern indicators. It is an internationally recognised qualification based on one-week training delivery and is facilitated via a five-day classroom/field-based delivery.

Key components include the following:

- Fire pattern indicator categories – identification and interpretation;
- Methodology – the process involved in investigating a wildfire scene;
- Fire scene evidence – protocols for gathering wildfire scene evidence;
- Witness interviewing – sourcing information about the fire from witnesses;
- Documentation – what and how do document a wildfire scene examination;
- Ignition factors and sources – recognised wildfire ignition sources and circumstances;
- Arson recognition – focus on specific issues around wildfire investigation and
- Court preparation and testimony – wildfire investigation-specific issues to ensure the success of legal proceedings in wildfire case preparation.

A fundamental learning outcome of this course involves the understanding of the formation and interpretation of fire pattern indicator categories as previously mentioned.

The 11 categories are as follows:

- Protection – occurs after one side of an object shields fuels from heat and flame;
- Grass stems – the position and condition of grass stems after impact by fire;
- Foliage freeze – foliage frozen in the direction of the wind or drafts after the passage of a fire front;
- Angle of char – the result of the interaction of fire on standing fuel such as trees or post resulting in a charred angle based on the direction of fire travel, slope and intensity;
- Spalling – fractured chips or shearing of flakes of the surface of rocks from the impact of an intense Advancing front of a wildfire;
- Curling* – the inward bending of leaves towards the heat source;
- Sooting – deposits of black carbon from incomplete combustion on the side of an object facing the approaching wildfire;
- Staining – deposits of resins and vaporised oils in flame and smoke on the surface of cooler objects;

Figure 8.3 Training Wildfire Investigators to identify ignition devices in FI-210 Wildland Fire Origin and Cause Determination Course, Guam, Mariana Islands (Photograph taken by the author).

- White ash deposits/formations – surfaces accumulating white ash formed from a fire edge;
- Cupping – formed on the ends of limbs and twigs after impact by a fire edge resulting in a cupped appearance and
- V- and U-patterns – the appearance of the fire's perimeter in the initial stages of wildfire progression from an ignition area (Figure 8.3).

(At the time of writing, this fire pattern indicator was under review and likely to be incorporated as a result of foliage freeze).*

Wildfire investigation team members

Under the Wildfire Investigation Incident Action Plan, investigators from representative agencies (specialists from, e.g. law enforcement, fire service, land management, county/local government) form the investigation team. Ideally, key members should have undertaken the FI-210 Wildland Fire Origin and Cause Determination Course, and all members should be trained in the NWCG 'FI-310 Wildland Fire Investigation Case Development Training Course'. The content of this course is restricted to those who attend as students due to the sensitive nature of the material. It is aimed at the investigation processes involved in undertaking a major or serial wildfire arson investigation, providing the skills to identify common trends in the occurrence of deliberately lit wildfires and proactive means to target wildfire arson in a collaborative approach. It is facilitated via a five-day classroom delivery, using a team approach working on an actual serial wildfire arson case.

Key components of this course include the following:

- Case documentation and organisation – identification, preparation and management of wildfire investigation documentation. Preparation of case material for legal proceedings;
- Behavioural evidence analysis – details the aspects of the tactical analysis of wildfire events, types of fire setters, motives and pattern analysis;
- Major wildfire investigation planning and management – details the aspects of investigation planning, the use of ICS (as depicted in Figure 8.4) in major wildfire investigations, pre-operational considerations; investigative tactics and resources to achieve investigation goals;
- Wildfire arson strategy and tactics – details an understanding and the relationship of tactics to strategy within a wildfire investigation. Practical application of a strategic operational plan using strategy and tactics;

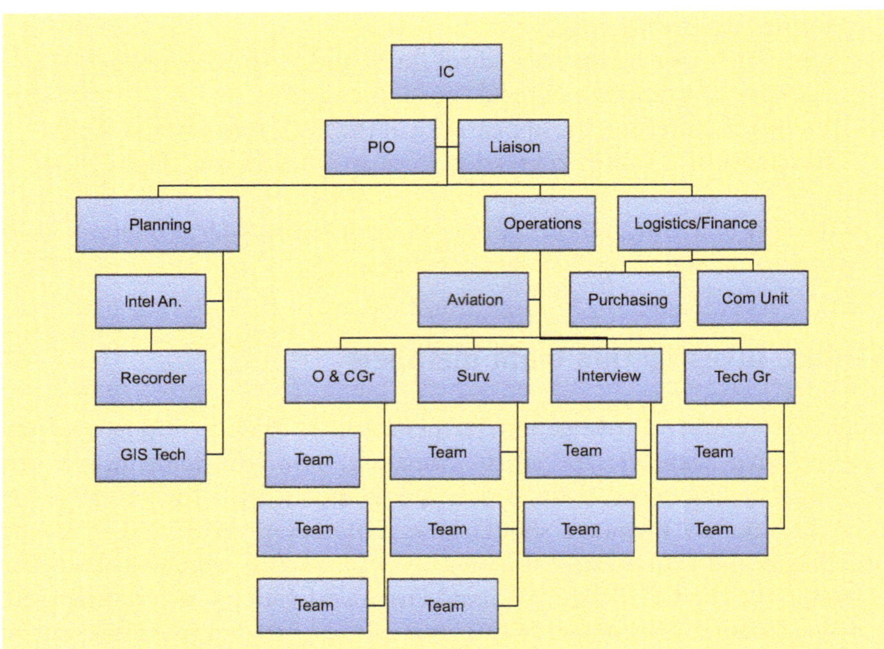

Figure 8.4 Investigation structure management training component of the FI-310 Wildland Fire Investigation Case Development Training Course (Used courtesy National Wildfire Co-ordinating Group, 2011).

- Physical evidence management – covers evidence management in a complex wildfire investigation, components of evidence management, expert witness abilities and specialities;
- Wildfire investigation forensic interviewing – specific to wildfire investigations, details the logistics and phases of law enforcement interviewing, preparation and planning for interviews, legal issues, phases of interviewing and specialist interviewing considerations;
- Search, seizure and arrest – aspects of wildfire investigation case law and legal issues relating to case-related search and seizures, aspects of the execution of warrants, along with considerations for the planning and execution of an arrest in wildfire investigations;
- Case presentation – how to prepare a case summary for presentation and how to manage wildfire case witnesses and
- Expert witness testimony – covers the role of expert witnesses and evidence testimony.

Who else can benefit from this specialist training?

Key officers involved in wildfire investigation cases such as agency lawyers, criminal prosecutors, GIS officers, criminal profilers and the like should also be considered for involvement in the FI-210 and FI-310 training courses. This provides the officers in these roles a greater understanding of wildfire arson investigation along with a complete appreciation of the terminology, methodology and specialist aspects involved. Experience has shown that providing these 'support roles' with these skills allows them to be more confident in contributing to the success of the investigation and prosecution of an arsonist. It is not considered practical for an investigator to deliver a 'last-minute' education to a prosecutor on the concepts of wildfire investigation and the range of terminologies used (Figure 8.5).

The Wildfire Arson Prevention Committee may also identify other specialist training opportunities for their Wildfire Investigation Team members, such as law enforcement–specific training in the use of surveillance technology such as unmanned aerial vehicles, access/interpretation of satellite images or use of Lidar equipment. The maintenance of skillsets should be a priority for the team members as technology and processes evolve in wildfire investigations.

Finally, the wildfire investigation training options outlined in this chapter are essential to provide the skills to officers to address the problem of wildfire arson. It is vital that officers who are likely to be involved with the tiered levels of wildfire suppression, wildfire scene examination, to team wildfire investigation roles, all receive this specialist training to confidently

Figure 8.5 Author providing cross-agency training of Wildfire Investigators in FI-210 Wildland Fire Origin and Cause Determination Course, Guam, Mariana Islands (photograph taken by Jeff Henricks, Canada).

and collaboratively address the problem of wildfire arson within their jurisdiction.

> Fire investigators must possess and maintain broad and up-to-date requisite knowledge and skills in their field.
>
> *(Icove & Haynes 2018, p. 2)*

References

Icove, D. & Haynes, G. (2018). *Kirks Fire Investigation* (8th edition). Pearson. New York, NY. USA.

National Wildfire Co-ordinating Group (2011). *FI-310 Wildland Fire Investigation; Case Development Course.* Boise, ID, USA.

9 Conclusion

The impact of serious wildfires on communities in wildfire-prone countries around the world is well known. When these impacts result from deliberate ignitions, the community is rightfully outraged. In more recent times, countries not normally known to be at risk from wildfire are now also being exposed to wildfire arson as their climates shift. As a result, strategies on how to deal with deliberate fire lighting need to be shared.

As highlighted in this guidebook, the challenge of solving the crime of wildfire arson requires a combined commitment from law enforcement, fire agencies, land management agencies and key government organisations who have a role in managing the protection of the community, spanning boundaries across the wildfire-prone landscape. To this end, the model of resource sharing and a team approach promoted in this guidebook is considered a constructive response by agencies to address the problem. Both small and large jurisdictions will benefit by establishing these formal arrangements.

With this in mind, it is important to recognise the investigation of wildfires can be ongoing, costly and challenging for the investigation teams involved, sometimes resulting in offenders not being apprehended. Senior officers from the Wildfire Arson Prevention Committee must, therefore, support this proactive approach by acknowledging that wildfire investigation cases may take many months or even years to resolve. However, without adopting an agreed strategy and having a collaborative approach, wildfire arson will continue to impact their communities.

Every deliberately lit wildfire event poses a risk. A small roadside wildfire can result in death or serious injury, when a responding fire service vehicle is involved in a motor vehicle accident, as firefighters extinguish the fire or to the crew of a responding firefighting aircraft. All are a risk to what may be perceived by an arsonist or emergency service managers, as a 'minor fire'.

If agency management adopts an attitude of ignorance or takes a stance suggesting that devoting resources to an ongoing investigation is too costly, they must be prepared to defend their inaction when a major fire results from the actions of a serial arsonist.

By accepting responsibility, working collaboratively across jurisdictional boundaries and following the intent detailed in this guidebook, the shared

DOI: 10.4324/9781003353843-10

problem of wildfire arson can become a shared solution. Without a proactive approach, wildfire arson, like any crime, will continue to cost the community and can eventually result in devastating consequences.

Figure 9.1 Photograph taken by the author.

Index

Note: *Italic* page numbers refer to figures.

ACT Rural Fire Service *1*
'Advancing Bushfire Arson Prevention Forum' *10*
aerial surveillance 68
aircraft/unmanned aerial vehicles 68
analysis of wildfire events: analysis process 50; buffer zone *52*, 54, *55*; crime circle hypothesis *52*, 54; distance decay 53; exclusion zone *52*, 56; in FI-310 training course 51; geospatial pattern analysis *51*, 52–53; ignition of wildfire to roadway *51*; information collation 47–50; modus operandi data 56; primary activity areas 54; secondary activity areas 56; signature analysis data 56–57; software programs 57; specialist roles 45–47; target selection data 56; temporal pattern analysis 52; wildfire scene investigation *49*
anger 9, *12*
arson recognition 64, 104
arson-related motives: crime concealment 8, 9, 86, 88; excitement 8, 9, 86; extremist/terrorism 8, 9, 86, 87; profit 8, 9, 86; revenge 8, 9, 86, 87; vandalism 8, 9, 86; *see also* wildfire arson
aviation observers 47

Behavioural Facet Model (Canter and Fritzon) 8
behavioural motive models, commonalities of 11–13
Bennett, Debra 8
'Black Summer' fire season *61*
Bryant, C. 3
buffer zone *52*, 54, *55*
Butry, D.T. 12

Calviño-Cancela, M. & Cañizo-Novelle, N. 13
Canter, D. 8; *Behavioural Facet Model* 8
Christensen, W. 23
circular expanding pattern 53, *53*
Clarke, R. V. 23
collaborative investigation approach: MAA SOPs 30–31, *31*; Memorandum of understanding (MOU) 29–30, *30*; Wildfire Arson Prevention Committee 28, *29*
collaborative wildfire investigation tactics: confidentiality 60; incident action plan 61–70; wildfire burning *61*; *see also* investigation approach
comfort zone *52*, 52–53
community engagement 73; general information sources 77, 80; rural area strategy 76–77; tactics 74–75; urban-interface area strategy 75–76, *76*; wildfire arson prevention messaging, examples of *78*, *79*; wildfire scene community information signage, example of *78*
confidentiality 60, *61*, 93
Cooksey, R. W. 8, 9
court preparation 64, 104
covert surveillance 47, 56, 70
crime circle hypothesis *52*, 53, 54
Crime Classification Manual (Douglas) 7–9
crime concealment 8, 9, 86, 88
crime stoppers information 69
crime triangle 21, *22*, 23

Davis, Michael 8
Depicker, A., De Baets, B., and Baetens, J.M. 3
digital tracking technology 47
distance decay 53

documentation 64, 65–66, 104
Doley, R.M. 13, 90; *The Psychology of Arson* 8
Douglas, J.E. 7, 9; *Crime Classification Manual* 7–9

Eck, J. 23
excitement 8, 9, 86
exclusion zone *52*, 56
'Extinguish Arson Intelligence Database' 57
extremism 8, 9, 86, 87

fire agencies: accidental 19; community engagement process 74, 83, 109; GAPP 34; hero status 86; investigating 62, 89, 98; leadership of 81; membership profiles 84; network of trust 93; officers or law enforcement 19, 28; reputation of 81; upgrading suppression resources 2; wildfire mitigation and property protection measures 74
fire behaviour and fire pattern indicators 62
Fire Danger Index 3
Fire Danger Rating 11
firefighter arson 9; first signs of 93–96, *96*; interviewing 98–99; issue of 82–84; lighting wildfires 84–89; media 92; prevention policy and tactics 89–93; screening of recruits 89–90; tactics for investigations 96–98; training 91–92; zero tolerance policy 91
fire scene evidence 64, 104
first responder and agency information sources 64–65, *65*
FI-110 Training Course *93*
FI-310 Training Course 51, 60, *106*, 107
'FI-210 Wildland Fire Origin and Cause Determination Course' 46, 103, *105*; aerial surveillance 68; arson recognition 64, 104; court preparation 64, 104; crime stoppers information 69; documentation 64, 104; documenting observers 65–66; fire behaviour and fire pattern indicators 62; fire scene evidence 64, 104; first responder and agency information sources 64–65, *65*; high-profile patrols 68–69; ignition factors and sources 64, 104; informants 69; interviews 66–68; license plate recognition cameras 68; media engagement 69; methodology 62–63; mobile surveillance 68; neighbourhood/area canvas 65; open-source analysis 68; physical evidence analysis 67; professional standards/investigator safety 62; search warrants 67–68; static surveillance via covert cameras 68; technical/electronic surveillance 68; use of polygraph testing 69–70; wildfire event analysis 66; wildfire K-9 teams 66, *66*; witness interviewing 64, 104
Fritzon, K. 8; *Behavioural Facet Model* 8

Ganteaume, A., Camia, A., Jappiot, M.; San-Miguel-Ayanz, J., Long-Fournel, M. & Lampin, C. 3, 4, 12, 14, 24, 50
Geographic Information System (GIS) Specialist 47
geospatial pattern analysis: circular expanding pattern 53, *53*; comfort zone *52*, 52–53; crime circle 53; linear expanding pattern 53, *54*; linear imploding pattern 53, *55*; multiple recurring 53, *55*; pattern types 53, *53*, *54*, *55*
'Gippsland Arson Prevention Program' (GAPP) 34
GPS surveillance monitoring 68

Hinds-Aldrich, M. 87, 89
Huff, T. 9, 82, 89

Icove, D. & Haynes, G. 45, 108
Ignition Area, defined as 63, 98
ignitions: accidental 17; agricultural or urban areas 24; arson 57, 69; in Belgium 3; circular expanding pattern *53*; consequence of human activity 3; Crime Circle of Activity *52*; delayed ignition device 85; deliberate wildfire 23, 75, 80, 109; early-stage wildfire *51*; factors and sources 64, 104; Fire Danger Rating 11; of fuels 46; lagged 57; linear expanding pattern *54*; linear imploding pattern *55*; location and recovery of evidence 47, *48*; locations at differing

times *55*; prevention strategy 13, 18, *19*; scattered 27; successful ignition 11, 23, 46, 56–57, 68, 73, *83*; timing of 3; unexplained increase 84; unplanned wildfires 1, 20; use of ignitable liquids 66; of vegetation fuels 73; wildfire progression 105, *105*
Incident Command System (ICS) 61
informants 69
information collation: cross-agency response protocol 48; extent of resourcing 47; fire cause information 47, 48, 49; jurisdictions 48; technical officers 47; timely and accurate identification of wildfire causes 48; triggers for scene examination 49, *49*; undetermined or accidental causes 47
information gathering process 47
information sharing and analysis: common operating platform program 32; establishment of secure website 31–32; evidence at wildfire scenes *33*; GAPP 34; 'living' document 35; MAA SOPs 34–35; silo-effect of wildfire event intelligence 32, 34; Victorian law enforcement 34; wildfire information exchange model *33*; Wildfire Investigation Incident Action Plans 35
intentional fires 12, 50
interviews 66–68
investigation approach: in addressing wildfire arson 19–22; collaborative investigation approach 28–31; and co-operation 28–36; firefighter arsonists 93–98; hidden problem of wildfire arson 18; incident action plan, tactical options in 61–70; information sharing and analysis 31–35; serial arson 22–25; wildfire 13, *14*; Wildfire Arson Prevention Committee, MOU, MAA SOPs, relationship of 35, *36*; Wildfire Ignition Prevention pie *19*; Wildfire Investigation Incident Action Plan *36*; wildfire scene *49*

Keeley, J.E., & Syphard, A.D. 24
Kocsis, R. N. 8, 9
K-9 (ignitable liquid detection and tracking) teams 47, 66, *66*

land management agencies 4, 28, 68, 103, 105, 109
law enforcement 4, 13, 18, 19, 28, 36, 89, 109; awareness campaigns 77; collaboration arrangements 92; corruption prevention policy 91; examining wildfire scene *30*; extended response times of 23; fire scene evidence 47; high-profile patrols 68; intelligence information 57; mainstream crimes 19; responsibility of 20; responsibility of catching offenders 2; specialist roles 97; suspicious persons and vehicles 74; training 101–102, 105, 107; use of polygraph testing 69–70; Victorian 34
license plate recognition cameras 68
Lindroth, R. 99
linear expanding pattern 53, *54*
linear imploding pattern 53, *55*
linkage blindness 20–21
local government 28, 34, 105
local Law Enforcement 28

MAA SOPs: best practice tactics 59; collaborative investigation approach 30–31, *31*; to overcome jurisdictional barriers 35
media engagement 69, 92
Memorandum of Understanding (MOU) 37; examining wildfire scene 30, *30*; specialist skillsets 29–30; Wildfire Arson Prevention Committee (Annexure A) 29, 38–39
mixed motives 88–89
mobile surveillance 68
modus operandi data 56
motives, arson 11–13
motive theory models, similarities between *12*
multiple recurring 53, *55*
Mutual Aid Agreement Standard Operating Procedures: example of (Annexure B) 41–43

National Fire Protection Association (NFPA) 5
National Interagency Fire Center (NIFC) 4
National Parks Service (NPS) 4
National Volunteer Fire Council 99

National Wildfire Co-ordinating Group (NWCG) 7; 'FI-310 Wildland Fire Investigation Case Development Course' 46, 59; 'FI-210 Wildland Fire Origin and Cause Determination Course' 46, 62–63
neighbourhood/area canvas 65
Nordskog, E. 60, 70, 90

O'Connor, J.J. 72
open-source analysis 68

patrols, high-profile 68–69
P.E.A.C.E model 67
physical evidence analysis 67
polygraph testing, use of 69–70
Prestemon, J.P. 12
primary activity areas 54
professional standards/investigator safety 62
profit 8, 9, 86
The Psychology of Arson (Doley) 8
pyromaniacs 7, 13

recruits, screening of 89–90
revenge 8, 9, 86, 87
risks of wildfire arson: education 18, *19*; enforcement 18, *19*; engineering 18, *19*; to life and property *4*; 'low-risk' events 3; in Netherlands *2*
routine activity theory 23
rural area strategy 76–77

search warrants 67–68
secondary activity areas 56
serial arson 22–25
sexual excitement 9, *12*
signature analysis data 56–57
silo effect 28, *29*
software programs 57
specialist roles: agency members of Wildfire Arson Prevention Committee 46; analysis of serial wildfire arson 45–46; experienced criminal analyst 46–47; experienced wildfire scene examination experts 46, *46*; GIS Specialist 47; investigation team members 47
State of Victoria's 'Operation Firesetter' strategy 34
static surveillance via covert cameras 68
Steensland, P. 21, 70, 83

target selection data 56
Teague, B., McLeod, R., and Pascoe, S. 34
technical/electronic surveillance 68
temporal pattern analysis 52
terrorism 8, 9, 86, 87
thrill 9, *12*
training: benefit from specialist training 107–108; competent wildfire scene examination *102*; cross-agency training *108*; firefighter arson 91–92; fire scene investigators 103–105; first-attending fire crews *103*; first response crews 102–103; identifying ignition devices *105*; investigation structure management training component *106*; is applicable 102; wildfire investigation team members 105–107

United States Fire Administration 9
urban-interface area strategy 75–76, *76*
US FBI National Centre for the Analysis of Violent Crime 8, 9

vandalism 8, 9, 86

wanton 9, *12*
wildfire arson: difficult to address 2; 'hidden problem' of 18; investigation challenge (*see* investigation approach); issue of 3–4; related motives (*see* arson-related motives); risk in Netherlands *2*
Wildfire Arson Prevention Committee 28; collaborative investigation approach 28, *29*
wildfire burning 60, *61*
wildfire event analysis 66
Wildfire Ignition Prevention pie 18, *19*
Wildfire Investigation Incident Action Plan (Annexure C) 35, *36*; best practice tactics 59; example of template 71–72; ICS structure, adoption of 61; safety of investigators 61–62; scene examinations 62–63, *63*, *64*, *65*, 65–68, *66*; tactical options in 61–70
witness interviewing 64, 104

zero tolerance policy 91

www.ingramcontent.com/pod-product-compliance
Ingram Content Group UK Ltd.
Pitfield, Milton Keynes, MK11 3LW, UK
UKHW051630200926
475701UK00015BB/910
9781032405940